Through which the unfenced footways pass,
Was law, and that which keeps the law,
Cherubic gaiety and awe;
Day was her doing, and the lark
Had reason for his song; the dark
In anagram innumerous spelt
Her name with stars that throbb'd and felt;
'Twas the sad summit of delight
To wake and weep for her at night;
She turn'd to triumph or to shame
The strife of every childish game;
The heart would come into my throat
At rosebuds; howsoe'er remote,
In opposition or consent,
Each thing, or person, or event,
Or seeming neutral howsoe'er,
All, in the live, electric air,
Awoke, took aspect, and confess'd
In her a centre of unrest,
Yea, stocks and stones within me bred
Anxieties of joy and dread.

O, bright apocalyptic sky
O'erarching childhood! Far and nigh
Mystery and obscuration none,
Yet nowhere any moon or sun!
What reason for these sighs? What hope,
Daunting with its audacious scope
The disconcerted heart, affects
These ceremonies and respects?
Why stratagems in everything?
Why, why not kiss her in the ring?
'Tis nothing strange that warriors bold,
Whose fierce, forecasting eyes behold
The city they desire to sack,
Humbly begin their proud attack
By delving ditches two miles off,
Aware how the fair place would scoff
At hasty wooing; but, O child,
Why thus approach thy playmate mild?

One morning, when it flush'd my thought
That, what in me such wonder wrought
Was call'd, in men and women, love,
And, sick with vanity thereof,
I, saying loud, 'I love her,' told
My secret to myself, behold
A crisis in my mystery!
For, suddenly, I seem'd to be
Whirl'd round, and bound with showers of threads
As when the furious spider sheds
Captivity upon the fly

To still his buzzing till he die;
Only, with me, the bonds that flew,
Enfolding, thrill'd me through and through
With bliss beyond aught heaven can have
And pride to dream myself her slave.

A long, green slip of wilder'd land,
With Knatchley Wood on either hand,
Sunder'd our home from hers. This day
Glad was I as I went her way.
I stretch'd my arms to the sky, and sprang
O'er the elastic sod, and sang
'I love her, love her!' to an air
Which with the words came then and there;
And even now, when I would know
All was not always dull and low,
I mind me awhile of the sweet strain
Love taught me in that lonely lane.

Such glories fade, with no more mark
Than when the sunset dies to dark.
They pass, the rapture and the grace
Ineffable, their only trace
A heart which, having felt no less
Than pure and perfect happiness,
Is duly dainty of delight;
A patient, poignant appetite
For pleasures that exceed so much
The poor things which the world calls such,
That, when these lure it, then you may
The lion with a wisp of hay.

That Charlotte, whom we scarcely knew
From Anne but by her ribbons blue,
Was loved, Anne less than look'd at, shows
That liking still by favour goes!
This Love is a Divinity,
And holds his high election free
Of human merit; or let's say,
A child by ladies call'd to play,
But careless of their becks and wiles,
Till, seeing one who sits and smiles
Like any else, yet only charms,
He cries to come into her arms.
Then, for my Cousins, fear me not!
None ever loved because he ought.
Fatal were else this graceful house,
So full of light from ladies' brows.
There's Mary; Heaven in her appears
Like sunshine through the shower's bright tears;
Mildred's of Earth, yet happier far
Than most men's thoughts of Heaven are;

The Victories Of Love by Coventry Patmore

Coventry Kersey Dighton Patmore was born on July 23rd 1823 at Woodford in Essex. Although he is still relatively unknown his stature as a Victorian Poet continues to increase.

Privately educated, Coventry was very close to his Father and inherited from him a love of literature.

His early ambition was to become an Artist and is 1838 he won the silver palette of the Society of Arts in 1838. The following year he was sent to France and here he began to write poems. On his return six months later his Father proposed to publish them but Coventry was now set upon a career as a scientist and the poems were set aside.

Thankfully it was not for long. As a great admirer of Tennyson he was inspired to return to writing and in 1844 he published a small volume of Poems. Although original the standard was uneven and it was not well received. Patmore acquired as many printed copies as he could and destroyed them. His friends continued to encourage him and this led to his introduction into the Pre-Raphaelite Brotherhood, contributing the poem "The Seasons" to The Germ.

His Father had by now fallen on harder times and in 1846 Coventry came to the post of printed book supernumary assistant at the British Museum, a post he occupied for nineteen years, devoting his spare time to poetry.

In 1847 he married Emily Andrews and she was to bear him two sons; Coventry (1848) and Tennyson (1850). Three daughters were to follow; Emily (1853), Bertha (1855) and Gertrude (1857), before Henry John was born in 1860.

In 1853 he was to republish Tamerton Church Tower, the more successful of his pieces from Poems of 1844, adding several new poems which showed the great strides he had made in both concept and execution. In 1854 the first part of his much loved The Angel in the House appeared.

In 1862 Emily died after a lengthy illness, and shortly afterwards Coventry turned to and joined the Roman Catholic church.

In 1865 he re-married to Marianne Byles. In 1877 he published The Unknown Eros, which contains his perhaps finest poetic work, and in the following year Amelia, his own favourite among his poems.

It is at this time that he also began to write essays beginning with English Metrical Law. Following this in 1879 with a volume of papers entitled Principle in Art, and in 1893 with Religio Poetae.

Tragically Marianne died in 1880, and in 1881 he married Harriet Robson. Their son Francis was born in 1882.

Coventry Patomre died at Lymington on November 26th 1896. He is buried in Lymington churchyard.

Index Of Contents

The Victories Of Love. Book I

I

From Frederick Graham

Mother, I smile at your alarms!
I own, indeed, my Cousin's charms,
But, like all nursery maladies,
Love is not badly taken twice.
Have you forgotten Charlotte Hayes,
My playmate in the pleasant days
At Knatchley, and her sister, Anne,
The twins, so made on the same plan,
That one wore blue, the other white,
To mark them to their father's sight;
And how, at Knatchley harvesting,
You bade me kiss her in the ring,
Like Anne and all the others? You,
That never of my sickness knew,
Will laugh, yet had I the disease,
And gravely, if the signs are these:

As, ere the Spring has any power,
The almond branch all turns to flower,
Though not a leaf is out, so she
The bloom of life provoked in me;
And, hard till then and selfish, I
Was thenceforth nought but sanctity
And service: life was mere delight
In being wholly good and right,
As she was; just, without a slur;
Honouring myself no less than her;
Obeying, in the loneliest place,
Ev'n to the slightest gesture, grace
Assured that one so fair, so true,
He only served that was so too.
For me, hence weak towards the weak,
No more the unnested blackbird's shriek
Startled the light-leaved wood; on high
Wander'd the gadding butterfly,
Unscared by my flung cap; the bee,
Rifling the hollyhock in glee,
Was no more trapp'd with his own flower,
And for his honey slain. Her power,
From great things even to the grass

But, for Honoria, Heaven and Earth
Seal'd amity in her sweet birth.
The noble Girl! With whom she talks
She knights first with her smile; she walks,
Stands, dances, to such sweet effect,
Alone she seems to move erect.
The brightest and the chastest brow
Rules o'er a cheek which seems to show
That love, as a mere vague suspense
Of apprehensive innocence,
Perturbs her heart; love without aim
Or object, like the sunlit flame
That in the Vestals' Temple glow'd,
Without the image of a god.
And this simplicity most pure
She sets off with no less allure
Of culture, subtly skill'd to raise
The power, the pride, and mutual praise
Of human personality
Above the common sort so high,
It makes such homely souls as mine
Marvel how brightly life may shine.
How you would love her! Even in dress
She makes the common mode express
New knowledge of what's fit so well
'Tis virtue gaily visible!
Nay, but her silken sash to me
Were more than all morality,
Had not the old, sweet, feverous ill
Left me the master of my will!

So, Mother, feel at rest, and please
To send my books on board. With these,
When I go hence, all idle hours
Shall help my pleasures and my powers.
I've time, you know, to fill my post,
And yet make up for schooling lost
Through young sea-service. They all speak
German with ease; and this, with Greek,
(Which Dr. Churchill thought I knew,)
And history, which I fail'd in too,
Will stop a gap I somewhat dread,
After the happy life I've led
With these my friends; and sweet 'twill be
To abridge the space from them to me.

II
From Mrs. Graham

My Child, Honoria Churchill sways
A double power through Charlotte Hayes.

In minds to first-love's memory pledged
The second Cupid's born full-fledged.
I saw, and trembled for the day
When you should see her beauty, gay
And pure as apple-blooms, that show
Outside a blush and inside snow,
Her high and touching elegance
Of order'd life as free as chance.
Ah, haste from her bewitching side,
No friend for you, far less a bride!
But, warning from a hope so wild,
I wrong you. Yet this know, my Child:
He that but once too nearly hears
The music of forefended spheres,
Is thenceforth lonely, and for all
His days like one who treads the Wall
Of China, and, on this hand, sees
Cities and their civilities,
And, on the other, lions. Well,
(Your rash reply I thus foretell,)
Good is the knowledge of what's fair,
Though bought with temporal despair!
Yes, good for one, but not for two.
Will it content a wife that you
Should pine for love, in love's embrace,
Through having known a happier grace;
And break with inward sighs your rest,
Because, though good, she's not the best?
You would, you think, be just and kind,
And keep your counsel! You will find
You cannot such a secret keep;
'Twill out, like murder, in your sleep;
A touch will tell it, though, for pride,
She may her bitter knowledge hide;
And, while she accepts love's make-believe,
You'll twice despise what you'd deceive.

I send the books. Dear Child, adieu!
Tell me of all you are and do.
I know, thank God, whate'er it be,
'Twill need no veil 'twixt you and me.

III
From Frederick

The multitude of voices blythe
Of early day, the hissing scythe
Across the dew drawn and withdrawn,
The noisy peacock on the lawn,
These, and the sun's eye-gladding gleam,
This morning, chased the sweetest dream

That e'er shed penitential grace
On life's forgetful commonplace;
Yet 'twas no sweeter than the spell
To which I woke to say farewell.

Noon finds me many a mile removed
From her who must not be beloved;
And us the waste sea soon shall part,
Heaving for aye, without a heart!
Mother, what need to warn me so?
I love Miss Churchill? Ah, no, no.
I view, enchanted, from afar,
And love her as I love a star,
For, not to speak of colder fear,
Which keeps my fancy calm, I hear,
Under her life's gay progress hurl'd,
The wheels of the preponderant world,
Set sharp with swords that fool to slay
Who blunders from a poor byway,
To covet beauty with a crown
Of earthly blessing added on;
And she's so much, it seems to me,
Beyond all women womanly,
I dread to think how he should fare
Who came so near as to despair.

IV
From Frederick

Yonder the sombre vessel rides
Where my obscure condition hides.
Waves scud to shore against the wind
That flings the sprinkling surf behind;
In port the bickering pennons show
Which way the ships would gladly go;
Through Edgecumb Park the rooted trees
Are tossing, reckless, in the breeze;
On top of Edgecumb's firm-set tower,
As foils, not foibles, of its power,
The light vanes do themselves adjust
To every veering of the gust:
By me alone may nought be given
To guidance of the airs of heaven?
In battle or peace, in calm or storm,
Should I my daily task perform,
Better a thousand times for love,
Who should my secret soul reprove?

Beholding one like her, a man
Longs to lay down his life! How can
Aught to itself seem thus enough,

When I have so much need thereof?
Blest in her place, blissful is she;
And I, departing, seem to be
Like the strange waif that comes to run
A few days flaming near the sun,
And carries back, through boundless night,
Its lessening memory of light.

Oh, my dear Mother, I confess
To a deep grief of homelessness,
Unfelt, save once, before. 'Tis years
Since such a shower of girlish tears
Disgraced me? But this wretched Inn,
At Plymouth, is so full of din,
Talkings and trampings to and fro.
And then my ship, to which I go
To-night, is no more home. I dread,
As strange, the life I long have led;
And as, when first I went to school,
And found the horror of a rule
Which only ask'd to be obey'd,
I lay and wept, of dawn afraid,
And thought, with bursting heart, of one
Who, from her little, wayward son,
Required obedience, but above
Obedience still regarded love,
So change I that enchanting place,
The abode of innocence and grace
And gaiety without reproof,
For the black gun-deck's louring roof,
Blind and inevitable law
Which makes light duties burdens, awe
Which is not reverence, laughters gain'd
At cost of purities profaned,
And whatsoever most may stir
Remorseful passion towards her,
Whom to behold is to depart
From all defect of life and heart.

But, Mother, I shall go on shore,
And see my Cousin yet once more!
'Twere wild to hope for her, you say.
I've torn and cast those words away.
Surely there's hope! For life 'tis well
Love without hope's impossible;
So, if I love, it is that hope
Is not outside the outer scope
Of fancy. You speak truth: this hour
I must resist, or lose the power.
What! and, when some short months are o'er,
Be not much other than before?
Drop from the bright and virtuous sphere

In which I'm held but while she's dear?
For daily life's dull, senseless mood,
Slay the fine nerves of gratitude
And sweet allegiance, which I owe
Whether the debt be weal or woe?
Nay, Mother, I, forewarn'd, prefer
To want for all in wanting her.

For all? Love's best is not bereft
Ever from him to whom is left
The trust that God will not deceive
His creature, fashion'd to believe
The prophecies of pure desire.
Not loss, not death, my love shall tire.
A mystery does my heart foretell;
Nor do I press the oracle
For explanations. Leave me alone,
And let in me love's will be done.

V
From Frederick

Fashion'd by Heaven and by art
So is she, that she makes the heart
Ache and o'erflow with tears, that grace
So lovely fair should have for place,
(Deeming itself at home the while,)
The unworthy earth! To see her smile
Amid this waste of pain and sin,
As only knowing the heaven within,
Is sweet, and does for pity stir
Passion to be her minister:
Wherefore last night I lay awake,
And said, 'Ah, Lord, for Thy love's sake,
Give not this darling child of Thine
To care less reverent than mine!'
And, as true faith was in my word,
I trust, I trust that I was heard.

The waves, this morning, sped to land,
And shouted hoarse to touch the strand,
Where Spring, that goes not out to sea,
Lay laughing in her lovely glee;
And, so, my life was sunlit spray
And tumult, as, once more to-day,
For long farewell did I draw near
My Cousin, desperately dear.
Faint, fierce, the truth that hope was none
Gleam'd like the lightning in the sun;
Yet hope I had, and joy thereof.
The father of love is hope, (though love

Lives orphan'd on, when hope is dead,)
And, out of my immediate dread
And crisis of the coming hour,
Did hope itself draw sudden power.
So the still brooding storm, in Spring,
Makes all the birds begin to sing.

Mother, your foresight did not err:
I've lost the world, and not won her.
And yet, ah, laugh not, when you think
What cup of life I sought to drink!
The bold, said I, have climb'd to bliss
Absurd, impossible, as this,
With nought to help them but so great
A heart it fascinates their fate.
If ever Heaven heard man's desire,
Mine, being made of altar-fire,
Must come to pass, and it will be
That she will wait, when she shall see,
This evening, how I go to get,
By means unknown, I know not yet
Quite what, but ground whereon to stand,
And plead more plainly for her hand!

And so I raved, and cast in hope
A superstitious horoscope!
And still, though something in her face
Portended 'No!' with such a grace
It burthen'd me with thankfulness,
Nothing was credible but 'Yes.'
Therefore, through time's close pressure bold,
I praised myself, and boastful told
My deeds at Acre; strain'd the chance
I had of honour and advance
In war to come; and would not see
Sad silence meant, 'What's this to me.'

When half my precious hour was gone,
She rose to greet a Mr. Vaughan;
And, as the image of the moon
Breaks up, within some still lagoon
That feels the soft wind suddenly,
Or tide fresh flowing from the sea,
And turns to giddy flames that go
Over the water to and fro,
Thus, when he took her hand to-night,
Her lovely gravity of light
Was scatter'd into many smiles
And flattering weakness. Hope beguiles
No more my heart, dear Mother. He,
By jealous looks, o'erhonour'd me.

With nought to do, and fondly fain
To hear her singing once again,
I stay'd, and turn'd her music o'er;
Then came she with me to the door.
'Dearest Honoria,' I said,
(By my despair familiar made,)
'Heaven bless you!' Oh, to have back then stepp'd
And fallen upon her neck, and wept,
And said, 'My friend, I owe you all
'I am, and have, and hope for. Call
'For some poor service; let me prove
'To you, or him here whom you love,
'My duty. Any solemn task,
'For life's whole course, is all I ask!'
Then she must surely have wept too,
And said, 'My friend, what can you do!'
And I should have replied, 'I'll pray
'For you and him three times a-day,
'And, all day, morning, noon, and night,
'My life shall be so high and right
'That never Saint yet scaled the stairs
'Of heaven with more availing prayers!'
But this (and, as good God shall bless
Somehow my end, I'll do no less,)
I had no right to speak. Oh, shame,
So rich a love, so poor a claim!

My Mother, now my only friend,
Farewell. The school-books which you send
I shall not want, and so return.
Give them away, or sell, or burn.
I'll write from Malta. Would I might
But be your little Child to-night,
And feel your arms about me fold,
Against this loneliness and cold!

VI
From Mrs. Graham

The folly of young girls! They doff
Their pride to smooth success, and scoff
At far more noble fire and might
That woo them from the dust of fight!

But, Frederick, now the storm is past,
Your sky should not remain o'ercast.
A sea-life's dull, and, oh, beware
Of nourishing, for zest, despair.
My Child, remember, you have twice
Heartily loved; then why not thrice,
Or ten times? But a wise man shuns

To cry 'All's over,' more than once.
I'll not say that a young man's soul
Is scarcely measure of the whole
Earthly and heavenly universe,
To which he inveterately prefers
The one beloved woman. Best
Speak to the senses' interest,
Which brooks no mystery nor delay:
Frankly reflect, my Son, and say,
Was there no secret hour, of those
Pass'd at her side in Sarum Close,
When, to your spirit's sick alarm,
It seem'd that all her marvellous charm
Was marvellously fled? Her grace
Of voice, adornment, movement, face
Was what already heart and eye
Had ponder'd to satiety;
And so the good of life was o'er,
Until some laugh not heard before,
Some novel fashion in her hair,
Or style of putting back her chair,
Restored the heavens. Gather thence
The loss-consoling inference.

Yet blame not beauty, which beguiles,
With lovely motions and sweet smiles,
Which while they please us pass away,
The spirit to lofty thoughts that stay
And lift the whole of after-life,
Unless you take the vision to wife,
Which then seems lost, or serves to slake
Desire, as when a lovely lake
Far off scarce fills the exulting eye
Of one athirst, who comes thereby,
And inappreciably sips
The deep, with disappointed lips.
To fail is sorrow, yet confess
That love pays dearly for success!
No blame to beauty! Let's complain
Of the heart, which can so ill sustain
Delight. Our griefs declare our fall,
But how much more our joys! They pall
With plucking, and celestial mirth
Can find no footing on the earth,
More than the bird of paradise,
Which only lives the while it flies.

Think, also, how 'twould suit your pride
To have this woman for a bride.
Whate'er her faults, she's one of those
To whom the world's last polish owes
A novel grace, which all who aspire

To courtliest custom must acquire.
The world's the sphere she's made to charm,
Which you have shunn'd as if 'twere harm.
Oh, law perverse, that loneliness
Breeds love, society success!
Though young, 'twere now o'er late in life
To train yourself for such a wife;
So she would suit herself to you,
As women, when they marry, do.
For, since 'tis for our dignity
Our lords should sit like lords on high,
We willingly deteriorate
To a step below our rulers' state;
And 'tis the commonest of things
To see an angel, gay with wings,
Lean weakly on a mortal's arm!
Honoria would put off the charm
Of lofty grace that caught your love,
For fear you should not seem above
Herself in fashion and degree,
As in true merit. Thus, you see,
'Twere little kindness, wisdom none,
To light your cot with such a sun.

VII
From Frederick

Write not, my Mother, her dear name
With the least word or hint of blame.
Who else shall discommend her choice,
I giving it my hearty voice?
Wed me? Ah, never near her come
The knowledge of the narrow home!
Far fly from her dear face, that shows
The sunshine lovelier than the rose,
The sordid gravity they wear
Who poverty's base burthen bear!
(And all are poor who come to miss
Their custom, though a crown be this.)
My hope was, that the wheels of fate,
For my exceeding need, might wait,
And she, unseen amidst all eyes,
Move sightless, till I sought the prize,
With honour, in an equal field.
But then came Vaughan, to whom I yield
With grace as much as any man,
In such cause, to another can.
Had she been mine, it seems to me
That I had that integrity
And only joy in her delight—
But each is his own favourite

In love! The thought to bring me rest
Is that of us she takes the best.

'Twas but to see him to be sure
That choice for her remain'd no more!
His brow, so gaily clear of craft;
His wit, the timely truth that laugh'd
To find itself so well express'd;
His words, abundant yet the best;
His spirit, of such handsome show
You mark'd not that his looks were so;
His bearing, prospects, birth, all these
Might well, with small suit, greatly please;
How greatly, when she saw arise
The reflex sweetness of her eyes
In his, and every breath defer
Humbly its bated life to her;
Whilst power and kindness of command,
Which women can no more withstand
Than we their grace, were still unquell'd,
And force and flattery both compell'd
Her softness! Say I'm worthy. I
Grew, in her presence, cold and shy.
It awed me, as an angel's might
In raiment of reproachful light.
Her gay looks told my sombre mood
That what's not happy is not good;
And, just because 'twas life to please,
Death to repel her, truth and ease
Deserted me; I strove to talk,
And stammer'd foolishness; my walk
Was like a drunkard's; if she took
My arm, it stiffen'd, ached, and shook:
A likely wooer! Blame her not;
Nor ever say, dear Mother, aught
Against that perfectness which is
My strength, as once it was my bliss.

And do not chafe at social rules.
Leave that to charlatans and fools.
Clay graffs and clods conceive the rose,
So base still fathers best. Life owes
Itself to bread; enough thereof
And easy days condition love;
And, kindly train'd, love's roses thrive,
No more pale, scentless petals five,
Which moisten the considerate eye
To see what haste they make to die,
But heavens of colour and perfume,
Which, month by month, renew the bloom
Of art-born graces, when the year
In all the natural grove is sere.

Blame nought then! Bright let be the air
About my lonely cloud of care.

VIII
From Frederick

Religion, duty, books, work, friends,—
'Tis good advice, but there it ends.
I'm sick for what these have not got.
Send no more books: they help me not;
I do my work: the void's there still
Which carefullest duty cannot fill.
What though the inaugural hour of right
Comes ever with a keen delight?
Little relieves the labour's heat;
Disgust oft crowns it when complete;
And life, in fact, is not less dull
For being very dutiful.
'The stately homes of England,' lo,
'How beautiful they stand!' They owe
How much to nameless things like me
Their beauty of security!
But who can long a low toil mend
By looking to a lofty end?
And let me, since 'tis truth, confess
The void's not fill'd by godliness.
God is a tower without a stair,
And His perfection, love's despair.
'Tis He shall judge me when I die;
He suckles with the hissing fly
The spider; gazes calmly down,
Whilst rapine grips the helpless town.
His vast love holds all this and more.
In consternation I adore.
Nor can I ease this aching gulf
With friends, the pictures of myself.

Then marvel not that I recur
From each and all of these to her.
For more of heaven than her have I
No sensitive capacity.
Had I but her, ah, what the gain
Of owning aught but that domain!
Nay, heaven's extent, however much,
Cannot be more than many such;
And, she being mine, should God to me
Say 'Lo! my Child, I give to thee
All heaven besides,' what could I then,
But, as a child, to Him complain
That whereas my dear Father gave

A little space for me to have
In His great garden, now, o'erblest,
I've that, indeed, but all the rest,
Which, somehow, makes it seem I've got
All but my only cared-for plot.
Enough was that for my weak hand
To tend, my heart to understand.

Oh, the sick fact, 'twixt her and me
There's naught, and half a world of sea.

IX
From Frederick

In two, in less than two hours more
I set my foot on English shore,
Two years untrod, and, strange to tell,
Nigh miss'd through last night's storm! There fell
A man from the shrouds, that roar'd to quench
Even the billows' blast and drench.
Besides me none was near to mark
His loud cry in the louder dark,
Dark, save when lightning show'd the deeps
Standing about in stony heaps.
No time for choice! A rope; a flash
That flamed as he rose; a dizzy splash;
A strange, inopportune delight
Of mounting with the billowy might,
And falling, with a thrill again
Of pleasure shot from feet to brain;
And both paced deck, ere any knew
Our peril. Round us press'd the crew,
With wonder in the eyes of most.
As if the man who had loved and lost
Honoria dared no more than that!

My days have else been stale and flat.
This life's at best, if justly scann'd,
A tedious walk by the other's strand,
With, here and there cast up, a piece
Of coral or of ambergris,
Which, boasted of abroad, we ignore
The burden of the barren shore.
I seldom write, for 'twould be still
Of how the nerves refuse to thrill;
How, throughout doubly-darken'd days,
I cannot recollect her face;
How to my heart her name to tell
Is beating on a broken bell;
And, to fill up the abhorrent gulf,
Scarce loving her, I hate myself.

Yet, latterly, with strange delight,
Rich tides have risen in the night,
And sweet dreams chased the fancies dense
Of waking life's dull somnolence.
I see her as I knew her, grace
Already glory in her face;
I move about, I cannot rest,
For the proud brain and joyful breast
I have of her. Or else I float,
The pilot of an idle boat,
Alone, alone with sky and sea,
And her, the third simplicity.
Or Mildred, to some question, cries,
(Her merry meaning in her eyes,)
'The Ball, oh, Frederick will go;
'Honoria will be there!' and, lo,
As moisture sweet my seeing blurs
To hear my name so link'd with hers,
A mirror joins, by guilty chance,
Either's averted, watchful glance!
Or with me, in the Ball-Room's blaze,
Her brilliant mildness thrids the maze;
Our thoughts are lovely, and each word
Is music in the music heard,
And all things seem but parts to be
Of one persistent harmony.
By which I'm made divinely bold;
The secret, which she knows, is told;
And, laughing with a lofty bliss
Of innocent accord, we kiss;
About her neck my pleasure weeps;
Against my lip the silk vein leaps;
Then says an Angel, 'Day or night,
'If yours you seek, not her delight,
'Although by some strange witchery
'It seems you kiss her, 'tis not she;
'But, whilst you languish at the side
'Of a fair-foul phantasmal bride,
'Surely a dragon and strong tower
'Guard the true lady in her bower.'
And I say, 'Dear my Lord, Amen!'
And the true lady kiss again.
Or else some wasteful malady
Devours her shape and dims her eye;
No charms are left, where all were rife,
Except her voice, which is her life,
Wherewith she, for her foolish fear,
Says trembling, 'Do you love me, Dear?'
And I reply, 'Sweetest, I vow
'I never loved but half till now.'
She turns her face to the wall at this,

And says, 'Go, Love, 'tis too much bliss.'
And then a sudden pulse is sent
About the sounding firmament
In smitings as of silver bars;
The bright disorder of the stars
Is solved by music; far and near,
Through infinite distinctions clear,
Their twofold voices' deeper tone
Utters the Name which all things own,
And each ecstatic treble dwells
On one whereof none other tells;
And we, sublimed to song and fire,
Take order in the wheeling quire,
Till from the throbbing sphere I start,
Waked by the heaving of my heart.

Such dreams as these come night by night,
Disturbing day with their delight.
Portend they nothing? Who can tell!
God yet may do some miracle.
'Tis nigh two years, and she's not wed,
Or you would know! He may be dead,
Or mad, and loving some one else,
And she, much moved that nothing quells
My constancy, or, simply wroth
With such a wretch, accept my troth
To spite him; or her beauty's gone,
(And that's my dream!) and this man Vaughan
Takes her release: or tongues malign,
Confusing every ear but mine,
Have smirch'd her: ah, 'twould move her, sure,
To find I loved her all the more!
Nay, now I think, haply amiss
I read her words and looks, and his,
That night! Did not his jealousy
Show—Good my God, and can it be
That I, a modest fool, all blest,
Nothing of such a heaven guess'd?
Oh, chance too frail, yet frantic sweet,
To-morrow sees me at her feet!

Yonder, at last, the glad sea roars
Along the sacred English shores!
There lies the lovely land I know,
Where men and women lordliest grow;
There peep the roofs where more than kings
Postpone state cares to country things,
And many a gay queen simply tends
The babes on whom the world depends;
There curls the wanton cottage smoke
Of him that drives but bears no yoke;
There laughs the realm where low and high

Are lieges to society.
And life has all too wide a scope,
Too free a prospect for its hope,
For any private good or ill,
Except dishonour, quite to fill!
—Mother, since this was penn'd, I've read
That 'Mr. Vaughan, on Tuesday, wed
'The beautiful Miss Churchill.' So
That's over; and to-morrow I go
To take up my new post on board
The 'Wolf,' my peace at last restored;
My lonely faith, like heart-of-oak,
Shock-season'd. Grief is now the cloak
I clasp about me to prevent
The deadly chill of a content
With any near or distant good,
Except the exact beatitude
Which love has shown to my desire.
Talk not of 'other joys and higher,'
I hate and disavow all bliss
As none for me which is not this.
Think not I blasphemously cope
With God's decrees, and cast off hope.
How, when, and where can mine succeed?
I'll trust He knows who made my need.

Baseness of men! Pursuit being o'er,
Doubtless her Husband feels no more
The heaven of heavens of such a Bride,
But, lounging, lets her please his pride
With fondness, guerdons her caress
With little names, and turns a tress
Round idle fingers. If 'tis so,
Why then I'm happier of the two!
Better, for lofty loss, high pain,
Than low content with lofty gain.
Poor, foolish Dove, to trust from me
Her happiness and dignity!

X
From Frederick

I thought the worst had brought me balm:
'Twas but the tempest's central calm.
Vague sinkings of the heart aver
That dreadful wrong is come to her,
And o'er this dream I brood and dote,
And learn its agonies by rote.
As if I loved it, early and late
I make familiar with my fate,
And feed, with fascinated will,

On very dregs of finish'd ill.
I think, she's near him now, alone,
With wardship and protection none;
Alone, perhaps, in the hindering stress
Of airs that clasp him with her dress,
They wander whispering by the wave;
And haply now, in some sea-cave,
Where the ribb'd sand is rarely trod,
They laugh, they kiss. Oh, God! oh, God!
There comes a smile acutely sweet
Out of the picturing dark; I meet
The ancient frankness of her gaze,
That soft and heart-surprising blaze
Of great goodwill and innocence,
And perfect joy proceeding thence!
Ah! made for earth's delight, yet such
The mid-sea air's too gross to touch.
At thought of which, the soul in me
Is as the bird that bites a bee,
And darts abroad on frantic wing,
Tasting the honey and the sting;
And, moaning where all round me sleep
Amidst the moaning of the deep,
I start at midnight from my bed—
And have no right to strike him dead.

What world is this that I am in,
Where chance turns sanctity to sin!
'Tis crime henceforward to desire
The only good; the sacred fire
That sunn'd the universe is hell!
I hear a Voice which argues well:
'The Heaven hard has scorn'd your cry;
'Fall down and worship me, and I
'Will give you peace; go and profane
'This pangful love, so pure, so vain,
'And thereby win forgetfulness
'And pardon of the spirit's excess,
'Which soar'd too nigh that jealous Heaven
'Ever, save thus, to be forgiven.
'No Gospel has come down that cures
'With better gain a loss like yours.
'Be pious! Give the beggar pelf,
'And love your neighbour as yourself!
'You, who yet love, though all is o'er,
'And she'll ne'er be your neighbour more,
'With soul which can in pity smile
'That aught with such a measure vile
'As self should be at all named 'love!'
'Your sanctity the priests reprove;
'Your case of grief they wholly miss;
'The Man of Sorrows names not this.

'The years, they say, graff love divine
'On the lopp'd stock of love like thine;
'The wild tree dies not, but converts.
'So be it; but the lopping hurts,
'The graff takes tardily! Men stanch
'Meantime with earth the bleeding branch,
'There's nothing heals one woman's loss,
'And lighten's life's eternal cross
'With intermission of sound rest,
'Like lying in another's breast.
'The cure is, to your thinking, low!
'Is not life all, henceforward, so?'

Ill Voice, at least thou calm'st my mood.
I'll sleep! But, as I thus conclude,
The intrusions of her grace dispel
The comfortable glooms of hell.

A wonder! Ere these lines were dried,
Vaughan and my Love, his three-days' Bride,
Became my guests. I look'd, and, lo,
In beauty soft as is the snow
And powerful as the avalanche,
She lit the deck. The Heav'n-sent chance!
She smiled, surprised. They came to see
The ship, not thinking to meet me.

At infinite distance she's my day:
What then to him? Howbeit they say
'Tis not so sunny in the sun
But men might live cool lives thereon!

All's well; for I have seen arise
That reflex sweetness of her eyes
In his, and watch'd his breath defer
Humbly its bated life to her,
His wife. My Love, she's safe in his
Devotion! What ask'd I but this?

They bade adieu; I saw them go
Across the sea; and now I know
The ultimate hope I rested on,
The hope beyond the grave, is gone,
The hope that, in the heavens high,
At last it should appear that I
Loved most, and so, by claim divine,
Should have her, in the heavens, for mine,
According to such nuptial sort
As may subsist in the holy court,
Where, if there are all kinds of joys
To exhaust the multitude of choice
In many mansions, then there are

Loves personal and particular,
Conspicuous in the glorious sky
Of universal charity,
As Phosphor in the sunrise. Now
I've seen them, I believe their vow
Immortal; and the dreadful thought,
That he less honour'd than he ought
Her sanctity, is laid to rest,
And, blessing them, I too am blest.
My goodwill, as a springing air,
Unclouds a beauty in despair;
I stand beneath the sky's pure cope
Unburthen'd even by a hope;
And peace unspeakable, a joy
Which hope would deaden and destroy,
Like sunshine fills the airy gulf
Left by the vanishing of self.
That I have known her; that she moves
Somewhere all-graceful; that she loves,
And is belov'd, and that she's so
Most happy, and to heaven will go,
Where I may meet with her, (yet this
I count but accidental bliss,)
And that the full, celestial weal
Of all shall sensitively feel
The partnership and work of each,
And thus my love and labour reach
Her region, there the more to bless
Her last, consummate happiness,
Is guerdon up to the degree
Of that alone true loyalty
Which, sacrificing, is not nice
About the terms of sacrifice,
But offers all, with smiles that say,
'Tis little, but it is for aye!

XI
From Mrs. Graham

You wanted her, my Son, for wife,
With the fierce need of life in life.
That nobler passion of an hour
Was rather prophecy than power;
And nature, from such stress unbent,
Recurs to deep discouragement.
Trust not such peace yet; easy breath,
In hot diseases, argues death;
And tastelessness within the mouth
Worse fever shows than heat or drouth.
Wherefore take, Frederick, timely fear
Against a different danger near:

Wed not one woman, oh, my Child,
Because another has not smiled!
Oft, with a disappointed man,
The first who cares to win him can;
For, after love's heroic strain,
Which tired the heart and brought no gain,
He feels consoled, relieved, and eased
To meet with her who can be pleased
To proffer kindness, and compute
His acquiescence for pursuit;
Who troubles not his lonely mood;
And asks for love mere gratitude.
Ah, desperate folly! Yet, we know,
Who wed through love wed mostly so.

At least, my Son, when wed you do,
See that the woman equals you,
Nor rush, from having loved too high,
Into a worse humility.
A poor estate's a foolish plea
For marrying to a base degree.
A woman grown cannot be train'd,
Or, if she could, no love were gain'd;
For, never was a man's heart caught
By graces he himself had taught.
And fancy not 'tis in the might
Of man to do without delight;
For, should you in her nothing find
To exhilarate the higher mind,
Your soul would deaden useless wings
With wickedness of lawful things,
And vampire pleasure swift destroy
Even the memory of joy.
So let no man, in desperate mood,
Wed a dull girl because she's good.
All virtues in his wife soon dim,
Except the power of pleasing him,
Which may small virtue be, or none!

I know my just and tender Son,
To whom the dangerous grace is given
That scorns a good which is not heaven;
My Child, who used to sit and sigh
Under the bright, ideal sky,
And pass, to spare the farmer's wheat,
The poppy and the meadow-sweet!
He would not let his wife's heart ache
For what was mainly his mistake;
But, having err'd so, all his force
Would fix upon the hard, right course.

She's graceless, say, yet good and true,

And therefore inly fair, and, through
The veils which inward beauty fold,
Faith can her loveliness behold.
Ah, that's soon tired; faith falls away
Without the ceremonial stay
Of outward loveliness and awe.
The weightier matters of the law
She pays: mere mint and cumin not;
And, in the road that she was taught,
She treads, and takes for granted still
Nature's immedicable ill;
So never wears within her eyes
A false report of paradise,
Nor ever modulates her mirth
With vain compassion of the earth,
Which made a certain happier face
Affecting, and a gayer grace
With pathos delicately edged!
Yet, though she be not privileged
To unlock for you your heart's delight,
(Her keys being gold, but not the right,)
On lower levels she may do!
Her joy is more in loving you
Than being loved, and she commands
All tenderness she understands.
It is but when you proffer more
The yoke weighs heavy and chafes sore.
It's weary work enforcing love
On one who has enough thereof,
And honour on the lowlihead
Of ignorance! Besides, you dread,
In Leah's arms, to meet the eyes
Of Rachel, somewhere in the skies,
And both return, alike relieved,
To life less loftily conceived.
Alas, alas!

Then wait the mood
In which a woman may be woo'd
Whose thoughts and habits are too high
For honour to be flattery,
And who would surely not allow
The suit that you could proffer now.
Her equal yoke would sit with ease;
It might, with wearing, even please,
(Not with a better word to move
The loyal wrath of present love);
She would not mope when you were gay,
For want of knowing aught to say;
Nor vex you with unhandsome waste
Of thoughts ill-timed and words ill-placed;
Nor reckon small things duties small,

And your fine sense fantastical;
Nor would she bring you up a brood
Of strangers bound to you by blood,
Boys of a meaner moral race,
Girls with their mother's evil grace,
But not her chance to sometimes find
Her critic past his judgment kind;
Nor, unaccustom'd to respect,
Which men, where 'tis not claim'd, neglect,
Confirm you selfish and morose,
And slowly, by contagion, gross;
But, glad and able to receive
The honour you would long to give,
Would hasten on to justify
Expectancy, however high,
Whilst you would happily incur
Compulsion to keep up with her.

XII
From Frederick

Your letter, Mother, bears the date
Of six months back, and comes too late.
My Love, past all conceiving lost,
A change seem'd good, at any cost,
From lonely, stupid, silent grief,
Vain, objectless, beyond relief,
And, like a sea-fog, settled dense
On fancy, feeling, thought, and sense.
I grew so idle, so despised
Myself, my powers, by Her unprized,
Honouring my post, but nothing more,
And lying, when I lived on shore,
So late of mornings: weak tears stream'd
For such slight cause,—if only gleam'd,
Remotely, beautifully bright,
On clouded eves at sea, the light
Of English headlands in the sun,—
That soon I deem'd 'twere better done
To lay this poor, complaining wraith
Of unreciprocated faith:
And so, with heart still bleeding quick,
But strengthen'd by the comfort sick
Of knowing that She could not care,
I turn'd away from my despair,
And told our chaplain's daughter, Jane,—
A dear, good girl, who saw my pain,
And look'd as if she pitied me,—
How glad and thankful I should be
If some kind woman, not above
Myself in rank, would give her love

To one that knew not how to woo.
Whereat she, without more ado,
Blush'd, spoke of love return'd, and closed
With what she thought I had proposed.

And, trust me, Mother, I and Jane,
We suit each other well. My gain
Is very great in this good Wife,
To whom I'm bound, for natural life,
By hearty faith, yet crossing not
My faith towards—I know not what!
As to the ether is the air,
Is her good to Honoria's fair;
One place is full of both, yet each
Lies quite beyond the other's reach
And recognition.

If you say,
Am I contented? Yea and nay!
For what's base but content to grow
With less good than the best we know?
But think me not from life withdrawn,
By passion for a hope that's gone,
So far as to forget how much
A woman is, as merely such,
To man's affection. What is best,
In each, belongs to all the rest;
And though, in marriage, quite to kiss
And half to love the custom is,
'Tis such dishonour, ruin bare,
The soul's interior despair,
And life between two troubles toss'd,
To me, who think not with the most;
Whatever 'twould have been, before
My Cousin's time, 'tis now so sore
A treason to the abiding throne
Of that sweet love which I have known,
I cannot live so, and I bend
My mind perforce to comprehend
That He who gives command to love
Does not require a thing above
The strength He gives. The highest degree
Of the hardest grace, humility;
The step t'ward heaven the latest trod,
And that which makes us most like God,
And us much more than God behoves,
Is, to be humble in our loves.
Henceforth for ever therefore I
Renounce all partiality
Of passion. Subject to control
Of that perspective of the soul
Which God Himself pronounces good,

Confirming claims of neighbourhood,
And giving man, for earthly life,
The closest neighbour in a wife,
I'll serve all. Jane be much more dear
Than all as she is much more near!
I'll love her! Yea, and love's joy comes
Ever from self-love's martyrdoms!

Yet, not to lie for God, 'tis true
That 'twas another joy I knew
When freighted was my heart with fire
Of fond, irrational desire
For fascinating, female charms,
And hopeless heaven in Her mild arms.
Nor wrong I any, if I profess
That care for heaven with me were less
But that I'm utterly imbued
With faith of all Earth's hope renew'd
In realms where no short-coming pains
Expectance, and dear love disdains
Time's treason, and the gathering dross,
And lasts for ever in the gloss
Of newness.

All the bright past seems,
Now, but a splendour in my dreams,
Which shows, albeit the dreamer wakes,
The standard of right life. Life aches
To be therewith conform'd; but, oh,
The world's so stolid, dark, and low!
That and the mortal element
Forbid the beautiful intent,
And, like the unborn butterfly,
It feels the wings, and wants the sky.

But perilous is the lofty mood
Which cannot yoke with lowly good.
Right life, for me, is life that wends
By lowly ways to lofty ends.
I well perceive, at length, that haste
T'ward heaven itself is only waste;
And thus I dread the impatient spur
Of aught that speaks too plain of Her.
There's little here that story tells;
But music talks of nothing else.
Therefore, when music breathes, I say,
(And urge my task,) Away, away!
Thou art the voice of one I knew,
But what thou say'st is not yet true;
Thou art the voice of her I loved,
And I would not be vainly moved.

So that which did from death set free
All things, now dons death's mockery,
And takes its place with things that are
But little noted. Do not mar
For me your peace! My health is high.
The proud possession of mine eye
Departed, I am much like one
Who had by haughty custom grown
To think gilt rooms, and spacious grounds,
Horses, and carriages, and hounds,
Fine linen, and an eider bed
As much his need as daily bread,
And honour of men as much or more.
Till, strange misfortune smiting sore,
His pride all goes to pay his debts,
A lodging anywhere he gets,
And takes his family thereto
Weeping, and other relics few,
Allow'd, by them that seize his pelf,
As precious only to himself.
Yet the sun shines; the country green
Has many riches, poorly seen
From blazon'd coaches; grace at meat
Goes well with thrift in what they eat;
And there's amends for much bereft
In better thanks for much that's left!

Jane is not fair, yet pleases well
The eye in which no others dwell;
And features somewhat plainly set,
And homely manners leave her yet
The crowning boon and most express
Of Heaven's inventive tenderness,
A woman. But I do her wrong,
Letting the world's eyes guide my tongue!
She has a handsomeness that pays
No homage to the hourly gaze,
And dwells not on the arch'd brow's height
And lids which softly lodge the light,
Nor in the pure field of the cheek
Flow'rs, though the soul be still to seek;
But shows as fits that solemn place
Whereof the window is the face:
Blankness and leaden outlines mark
What time the Church within is dark;
Yet view it on a Festal night,
Or some occasion else for light,
And each ungainly line is seen
A special character to mean
Of Saint or Prophet, and the whole
Blank window is a living scroll.

For hours, the clock upon the shelf,
Has all the talking to itself;
But to and fro her needle runs
Twice, while the clock is ticking once;
And, when a wife is well in reach,
Not silence separates, but speech;
And I, contented, read, or smoke,
And idly think, or idly stroke
The winking cat, or watch the fire,
In social peace that does not tire;
Until, at easeful end of day,
She moves, and puts her work away,
And, saying 'How cold 'tis,' or 'How warm,'
Or something else as little harm,
Comes, used to finding, kindly press'd,
A woman's welcome to my breast,
With all the great advantage clear
Of none else having been so near.

But sometimes, (how shall I deny!)
There falls, with her thus fondly by,
Dejection, and a chilling shade.
Remember'd pleasures, as they fade,
Salute me, and colossal grow,
Like foot-prints in the thawing snow.
I feel oppress'd beyond my force
With foolish envy and remorse.
I love this woman, but I might
Have loved some else with more delight;
And strange it seems of God that He
Should make a vain capacity.

Such times of ignorant relapse,
'Tis well she does not talk, perhaps.
The dream, the discontent, the doubt,
To some injustice flaming out,
Were't else, might leave us both to moan
A kind tradition overthrown,
And dawning promise once more dead
In the pernicious lowlihead
Of not aspiring to be fair.
And what am I, that I should dare
Dispute with God, who moulds one clay
To honour and shame, and wills to pay
With equal wages them that delve
About His vines one hour or twelve!

XIII
From Lady Clitheroe To Mary Churchill

I've dreadful news, my Sister dear!

Frederick has married, as we hear,
Oh, such a girl! This fact we get
From Mr. Barton, whom we met
At Abury once. He used to know,
At Race and Hunt, Lord Clitheroe,
And writes that he 'has seen Fred Graham,
'Commander of the 'Wolf,'—the same
'The Mess call'd Joseph,—with his Wife
'Under his arm.' He 'lays his life,
'The fellow married her for love,
'For there was nothing else to move.
'H. is her Shibboleth. 'Tis said
'Her Mother was a Kitchen-Maid.'

Poor Fred! What will Honoria say?
She thought so highly of him. Pray
Tell it her gently. I've no right,
I know you hold, to trust my sight;
But Frederick's state could not be hid!
And Felix, coming when he did,
Was lucky; for Honoria, too,
Was half in love. How warm she grew
On 'worldliness,' when once I said
I fancied that, in ladies, Fred
Had tastes much better than his means!
His hand was worthy of a Queen's,
Said she, and actually shed tears
The night he left us for two years,
And sobb'd, when ask'd the cause to tell,
That 'Frederick look'd so miserable.'
He did look very dull, no doubt,
But such things girls don't cry about.

What weathercocks men always prove!
You're quite right not to fall in love.
I never did, and, truth to tell,
I don't think it respectable.
The man can't understand it, too.
He likes to be in love with you,
But scarce knows how, if you love him,
Poor fellow. When 'tis woman's whim
To serve her husband night and day,
The kind soul lets her have her way!
So, if you wed, as soon you should,
Be selfish for your husband's good.
Happy the men who relegate
Their pleasures, vanities, and state
To us. Their nature seems to be
To enjoy themselves by deputy,
For, seeking their own benefit,
Dear, what a mess they make of it!
A man will work his bones away,

If but his wife will only play;
He does not mind how much he's teased,
So that his plague looks always pleased;
And never thanks her, while he lives,
For anything, but what he gives!
'Tis hard to manage men, we hear!
Believe me, nothing's easier, Dear.
The most important step by far
Is finding what their colours are.
The next is, not to let them know
The reason why they love us so.
The indolent droop of a blue shawl,
Or gray silk's fluctuating fall,
Covers the multitude of sins
In me. Your husband, Love, might wince
At azure, and be wild at slate,
And yet do well with chocolate.
Of course you'd let him fancy he
Adored you for your piety.

XIV
From Jane To Her Mother

Dear Mother, as you write, I see
How glad and thankful I should be
For such a husband. Yet to tell
The truth, I am so miserable!
How could he—I remember, though,
He never said he loved me! No,
He is so right that all seems wrong
I've done and thought my whole life long!
I'm grown so dull and dead with fear
That Yes and No, when he is near,
Is all I have to say. He's quite
Unlike what most would call polite,
And yet, when first I saw him come
To tea in Aunt's fine drawing-room,
He made me feel so common! Oh,
How dreadful if he thinks me so!
It's no use trying to behave
To him. His eye, so kind and grave,
Sees through and through me! Could not you,
Without his knowing that I knew,
Ask him to scold me now and then?
Mother, it's such a weary strain
The way he has of treating me
As if 'twas something fine to be
A woman; and appearing not
To notice any faults I've got!
I know he knows I'm plain, and small,
Stupid, and ignorant, and all

Awkward and mean; and, by degrees,
I see a beauty which he sees,
When often he looks strange awhile,
Then recollects me with a smile.

I wish he had that fancied Wife,
With me for Maid, now! all my life
To dress her out for him, and make
Her looks the lovelier for his sake;
To have her rate me till I cried;
Then see her seated by his side,
And driven off proudly to the Ball;
Then to stay up for her, whilst all
The servants were asleep; and hear
At dawn the carriage rolling near,
And let them in; and hear her laugh,
And boast, he said that none was half
So beautiful, and that the Queen,
Who danced with him the first, had seen
And noticed her, and ask'd who was
That lady in the golden gauze?
And then to go to bed, and lie
In a sort of heavenly jealousy,
Until 'twas broad day, and I guess'd
She slept, nor knew how she was bless'd.

Pray burn this letter. I would not
Complain, but for the fear I've got
Of going wild, as we hear tell
Of people shut up in a cell,
With no one there to talk to. He
Must never know he is loved by me
The most; he'd think himself to blame;
And I should almost die for shame.

If being good would serve instead
Of being graceful, ah, then, Fred—
But I, myself, I never could
See what's in women's being good;
For all their goodness is to do
Just what their nature tells them to.
Now, when a man would do what's right,
He has to try with all his might.

Though true and kind in deed and word,
Fred's not a vessel of the Lord.
But I have hopes of him; for, oh,
How can we ever surely know
But that the very darkest place
May be the scene of saving grace!

XV
From Frederick

'How did I feel?' The little wight
Fill'd me, unfatherly, with fright!
So grim it gazed, and, out of the sky,
There came, minute, remote, the cry,
Piercing, of original pain.
I put the wonder back to Jane,
And her delight seem'd dash'd, that I,
Of strangers still by nature shy,
Was not familiar quite so soon
With her small friend of many a moon.
But, when the new-made Mother smiled,
She seem'd herself a little child,
Dwelling at large beyond the law
By which, till then, I judged and saw;
And that fond glow which she felt stir
For it, suffused my heart for her;
To whom, from the weak babe, and thence
To me, an influent innocence,
Happy, reparative of life,
Came, and she was indeed my wife,
As there, lovely with love she lay,
Brightly contented all the day
To hug her sleepy little boy,
In the reciprocated joy
Of touch, the childish sense of love,
Ever inquisitive to prove
Its strange possession, and to know
If the eye's report be really so.

XVI
From Jane To Mrs. Graham

Dear Mother,—such if you'll allow,
In love, not law, I'll call you now,—
I hope you're well. I write to say
Frederick has got, besides his pay,
A good appointment in the Docks;
Also to thank you for the frocks
And shoes for Baby. I, (D.V.,)
Shall soon be strong. Fred goes to sea
No more. I am so glad; because,
Though kinder husband never was,
He seems still kinder to become
The more he stays with me at home.
When we are parted, I see plain
He's dull till he gets used again
To marriage. Do not tell him, though;
I would not have him know I know,

For all the world.

I try to mind
All your advice; but sometimes find
I do not well see how. I thought
To take it about dress; so bought
A gay new bonnet, gown, and shawl;
But Frederick was not pleased at all;
For, though he smiled, and said, 'How smart!'
I feel, you know, what's in his heart.
But I shall learn! I fancied long
That care in dress was very wrong,
Till Frederick, in his startling way,
When I began to blame, one day,
The Admiral's Wife, because we hear
She spends two hours, or something near,
In dressing, took her part, and said
How all things deck themselves that wed;
How birds and plants grow fine to please
Each other in their marriages;
And how (which certainly is true—
It never struck me—did it you?)
Dress was, at first, Heaven's ordinance,
And has much Scripture countenance.
For Eliezer, we are told,
Adorn'd with jewels and with gold
Rebecca. In the Psalms, again,
How the King's Daughter dress'd! And, then,
The Good Wife in the Proverbs, she
Made herself clothes of tapestry,
Purple and silk: and there's much more
I had not thought about before!
But Fred's so clever! Do you know,
Since Baby came, he loves me so!
I'm really useful, now, to Fred;
And none could do so well instead.
It's nice to fancy, if I died,
He'd miss me from the Darling's side!
Also, there's something now, you see,
On which we talk, and quite agree;
On which, without pride too, I can
Hope I'm as wise as any man.
I should be happy now, if quite
Sure that in one thing Fred was right.
But, though I trust his prayers are said,
Because he goes so late to bed,
I doubt his Calling. Glad to find
A text adapted to his mind,—
That where St. Paul, in Man and Wife,
Allows a little worldly life,—
He smiled, and said that he knew all
Such things as that without St. Paul!

And once he said, when I with pain
Had got him just to read Romaine,
'Men's creeds should not their hopes condemn.
'Who wait for heaven to come to them
'Are little like to go to heaven,
'If logic's not the devil's leaven!'
I cried at such a wicked joke,
And he, surprised, went out to smoke.

But to judge him is not for me,
Who myself sin so dreadfully
As half to doubt if I should care
To go to heaven, and he not there.
He must be right; and I dare say
I shall soon understand his way.
To other things, once strange, I've grown
Accustom'd, nay, to like. I own
'Twas long before I got well used
To sit, while Frederick read or mused
For hours, and scarcely spoke. When he
For all that, held the door to me,
Pick'd up my handkerchief, and rose
To set my chair, with other shows
Of honour, such as men, 'tis true,
To sweethearts and fine ladies do,
It almost seem'd an unkind jest;
But now I like these ways the best.
They somehow make me gentle and good;
And I don't mind his quiet mood.
If Frederick does seem dull awhile,
There's Baby. You should see him smile!
I'm pretty and nice to him, sweet Pet,
And he will learn no better yet:
Indeed, now little Johnny makes
A busier time of it, and takes
Our thoughts off one another more,
I'm happy as need be, I'm sure!

XVII
From Felix To Honoria

Let me, Beloved, while gratitude
Is garrulous with coming good,
Or ere the tongue of happiness
Be silenced by your soft caress,
Relate how, musing here of you,
The clouds, the intermediate blue,
The air that rings with larks, the grave
And distant rumour of the wave,
The solitary sailing skiff,
The gusty corn-field on the cliff,

The corn-flower by the crumbling ledge,
Or, far-down at the shingle's edge,
The sighing sea's recurrent crest
Breaking, resign'd to its unrest,
All whisper, to my home-sick thought,
Of charms in you till now uncaught,
Or only caught as dreams, to die
Ere they were own'd by memory.

High and ingenious Decree
Of joy-devising Deity!
You whose ambition only is
The assurance that you make my bliss,
(Hence my first debt of love to show,
That you, past showing, indeed do so!)
Trust me, the world, the firmament,
With diverse-natured worlds besprent,
Were rear'd in no mere undivine
Boast of omnipotent design,
The lion differing from the snake
But for the trick of difference sake,
And comets darting to and fro
Because in circles planets go;
But rather that sole love might be
Refresh'd throughout eternity
In one sweet faith, for ever strange,
Mirror'd by circumstantial change.
For, more and more, do I perceive
That everything is relative
To you, and that there's not a star,
Nor nothing in't, so strange or far,
But, if 'twere scanned, 'twould chiefly mean
Somewhat, till then, in you unseen,
Something to make the bondage strait
Of you and me more intimate,
Some unguess'd opportunity
Of nuptials in a new degree.

But, oh, with what a novel force
Your best-conn'd beauties, by remorse
Of absence, touch; and, in my heart,
How bleeds afresh the youthful smart
Of passion fond, despairing still
To utter infinite good-will
By worthy service! Yet I know
That love is all that love can owe,
And this to offer is no less
Of worth, in kind speech or caress,
Than if my life-blood I should give.
For good is God's prerogative,
And Love's deed is but to prepare
The flatter'd, dear Belov'd to dare

Acceptance of His gifts. When first
On me your happy beauty burst,
Honoria, verily it seem'd
That naught beyond you could be dream'd
Of beauty and of heaven's delight.
Zeal of an unknown infinite
Yet bade me ever wish you more
Beatified than e'er before.
Angelical were your replies
To my prophetic flatteries;
And sweet was the compulsion strong
That drew me in the course along
Of heaven's increasing bright allure,
With provocations fresh of your
Victorious capacity.
Whither may love, so fledged, not fly?

Did not mere Earth hold fast the string
Of this celestial soaring thing,
So measure and make sensitive,
And still, to the nerves, nice notice give
Of each minutest increment
Of such interminable ascent,
The heart would lose all count, and beat
Unconscious of a height so sweet,
And the spirit-pursuing senses strain
Their steps on the starry track in vain!
But, reading now the note just come,
With news of you, the babes, and home,
I think, and say, 'To-morrow eve
'With kisses me will she receive;'
And, thinking, for extreme delight
Of love's extremes, I laugh outright.

XVIII
From Frederick

Eight wedding-days gone by, and none
Yet kept, to keep them all in one,
Jane and myself, with John and Grace
On donkeys, visited the place
I first drew breath in, Knatchley Wood.
Bearing the basket, stuff'd with food,
Milk, loaves, hard eggs, and marmalade,
I halted where the wandering glade
Divides the thicket. There I knew,
It seem'd, the very drops of dew
Below the unalter'd eglantine.
Nothing had changed since I was nine!

In the green desert, down to eat

We sat, our rustic grace at meat
Good appetite, through that long climb
Hungry two hours before the time.
And there Jane took her stitching out,
And John for birds'-nests pry'd about,
And Grace and Baby, in between
The warm blades of the breathing green,
Dodged grasshoppers; and I no less,
In conscientious idleness,
Enjoy'd myself, under the noon
Stretch'd, and the sounds and sights of June
Receiving, with a drowsy charm,
Through muffled ear and folded arm.

And then, as if I sweetly dream'd,
I half-remember'd how it seem'd
When I, too, was a little child
About the wild wood roving wild.
Pure breezes from the far-off height
Melted the blindness from my sight,
Until, with rapture, grief, and awe,
I saw again as then I saw.
As then I saw, I saw again
The harvest-waggon in the lane,
With high-hung tokens of its pride
Left in the elms on either side;
The daisies coming out at dawn
In constellations on the lawn;
The glory of the daffodil;
The three black windmills on the hill,
Whose magic arms, flung wildly by,
Sent magic shadows o'er the rye.
Within the leafy coppice, lo,
More wealth than miser's dreams could show,
The blackbird's warm and woolly brood,
Five golden beaks agape for food;
The Gipsies, all the summer seen
Native as poppies to the Green;
The winter, with its frosts and thaws
And opulence of hips and haws;
The lovely marvel of the snow;
The Tamar, with its altering show
Of gay ships sailing up and down,
Among the fields and by the Town;
And, dearer far than anything,
Came back the songs you used to sing.
(Ah, might you sing such songs again,
And I, your Child, but hear as then,
With conscious profit of the gulf
Flown over from my present self!)
And, as to men's retreating eyes,
Beyond high mountains higher rise,

Still farther back there shone to me
The dazzling dusk of infancy.
Thither I look'd, as, sick of night,
The Alpine shepherd looks to the height,
And does not see the day, 'tis true,
But sees the rosy tops that do.

Meantime Jane stitch'd, and fann'd the flies
From my repose, with hush'd replies
To Grace, and smiles when Baby fell.
Her countenance love visible
Appear'd, love audible her voice.
Why in the past alone rejoice,
Whilst here was wealth before me cast
Which, I could feel, if 'twere but past
Were then most precious? Question vain,
When ask'd again and yet again,
Year after year; yet now, for no
Cause, but that heaven's bright winds will blow
Not at our pray'r but as they list,
It brought that distant, golden mist
To grace the hour, firing the deep
Of spirit and the drowsy keep
Of joy, till, spreading uncontain'd,
The holy power of seeing gain'd
The outward eye, this owning even
That where there's love and truth there's heaven.

Debtor to few, forgotten hours
Am I, that truths for me are powers.
Ah, happy hours, 'tis something yet
Not to forget that I forget!

And now a cloud, bright, huge and calm,
Rose, doubtful if for bale or balm;
O'ertoppling towers and bulwarks bright
Appear'd, at beck of viewless might,
Along a rifted mountain range.
Untraceable and swift in change,
Those glittering peaks, disrupted, spread
To solemn bulks, seen overhead;
The sunshine quench'd, from one dark form
Fumed the appalling light of storm.
Straight to the zenith, black with bale,
The Gipsies' smoke rose deadly pale;
And one wide night of hopeless hue
Hid from the heart the recent blue.
And soon, with thunder crackling loud,
A flash reveal'd the formless cloud:
Lone sailing rack, far wavering rim,
And billowy tracks of stormland dim.

We stood, safe group'd beneath a shed.
Grace hid behind Jane's gown for dread,
Who told her, fondling with her hair,
'The naughty noise! but God took care
'Of all good girls.' John seem'd to me
Too much for Jane's theology,
Who bade him watch the tempest. Now
A blast made all the woodland bow;
Against the whirl of leaves and dust
Kine dropp'd their heads; the tortured gust
Jagg'd and convuls'd the ascending smoke
To mockery of the lightning's stroke.
The blood prick'd, and a blinding flash
And close coinstantaneous crash
Humbled the soul, and the rain all round
Resilient dimm'd the whistling ground,
Nor flagg'd in force from first to last,
Till, sudden as it came, 'twas past,
Leaving a trouble in the copse
Of brawling birds and tinkling drops.

Change beyond hope! Far thunder faint
Mutter'd its vast and vain complaint,
And gaps and fractures, fringed with light,
Show'd the sweet skies, with squadrons bright
Of cloudlets, glittering calm and fair
Through gulfs of calm and glittering air.

With this adventure, we return'd.
The roads the feet no longer burn'd.
A wholesome smell of rainy earth
Refresh'd our spirits, tired of mirth.
The donkey-boy drew friendly near
My Wife, and, touch'd by the kind cheer
Her countenance show'd, or sooth'd perchance
By the soft evening's sad advance,
As we were, stroked the flanks and head
Of the ass, and, somewhat thick-voiced, said,
'To 'ave to wop the donkeys so
''Ardens the 'art, but they won't go
'Without!' My Wife, by this impress'd,
As men judge poets by their best,
When now we reach'd the welcome door,
Gave him his hire, and sixpence more.

XIX
From Jane

Dear Mrs. Graham, the fever's past,
And Fred is well. I, in my last,
Forgot to say that, while 'twas on,

A lady, call'd Honoria Vaughan,
One of his Salisbury Cousins, came.
Had I, she ask'd me, heard her name?
'Twas that Honoria, no doubt,
Whom he would sometimes talk about
And speak to, when his nights were bad,
And so I told her that I had.

She look'd so beautiful and kind!
And just the sort of wife my mind
Pictured for Fred, with many tears,
In those sad early married years.

Visiting, yesterday, she said,
The Admiral's Wife, she learn'd that Fred
Was very ill; she begg'd to be,
If possible, of use to me.
What could she do? Last year, his Aunt
Died, leaving her, who had no want,
Her fortune. Half was his, she thought;
But he, she knew, would not be brought
To take his rights at second hand.
Yet something might, she hoped, be plann'd.
What did I think of putting John
To school and college? Mr. Vaughan,
When John was old enough, could give
Preferment to her relative;
And she should be so pleased.—I said
I felt quite sure that dearest Fred
Would be most thankful. Would we come,
And make ourselves, she ask'd, at home,
Next month, at High-Hurst? Change of air
Both he and I should need, and there
At leisure we could talk, and then
Fix plans, as John was nearly ten.

It seemed so rude to think and doubt,
So I said, Yes. In going out,
She said, 'How strange of Frederick, Dear,'
(I wish he had been there to hear,)
'To send no cards, or tell me what
'A nice new Cousin I had got!'
Was not that kind?

When Fred grew strong,
I had, I found, done very wrong.
Anger was in his voice and eye.
With people born and bred so high
As Fred and Mrs. Vaughan and you,
It's hard to guess what's right to do;
And he won't teach me!

Dear Fred wrote,
Directly, such a lovely note,
Which, though it undid all I had done,
Was, both to me and Mrs. Vaughan,
So kind! His words, I can't say why,
Like soldiers' music, made me cry.

The Victories Of Love. Book II
I
From Jane To Her Mother

Thank Heaven, the burthens on the heart
Are not half known till they depart!
Although I long'd, for many a year,
To love with love that casts out fear,
My Frederick's kindness frighten'd me,
And heaven seem'd less far off than he;
And in my fancy I would trace
A lady with an angel's face,
That made devotion simply debt,
Till sick with envy and regret,
And wicked grief that God should e'er
Make women, and not make them fair.
That he might love me more because
Another in his memory was,
And that my indigence might be
To him what Baby's was to me,
The chief of charms, who could have thought?
But God's wise way is to give nought
Till we with asking it are tired;
And when, indeed, the change desired
Comes, lest we give ourselves the praise,
It comes by Providence, not Grace;
And mostly our thanks for granted pray'rs
Are groans at unexpected cares.
First Baby went to heaven, you know,
And, five weeks after, Grace went, too.
Then he became more talkative,
And, stooping to my heart, would give
Signs of his love, which pleased me more
Than all the proofs he gave before;
And, in that time of our great grief,
We talk'd religion for relief;
For, though we very seldom name
Religion, we now think the same!
Oh, what a bar is thus removed
To loving and to being loved!
For no agreement really is
In anything when none's in this.
Why, Mother, once, if Frederick press'd
His wife against his hearty breast,

The interior difference seem'd to tear
My own, until I could not bear
The trouble. 'Twas a dreadful strife,
And show'd, indeed, that faith is life.
He never felt this. If he did,
I'm sure it could not have been hid;
For wives, I need not say to you,
Can feel just what their husbands do,
Without a word or look; but then
It is not so, you know, with men.

From that time many a Scripture text
Help'd me, which had, before, perplex'd.
Oh, what a wond'rous word seem'd this:
He is my head, as Christ is his!
None ever could have dared to see
In marriage such a dignity
For man, and for his wife, still less,
Such happy, happy lowliness,
Had God Himself not made it plain!
This revelation lays the rein—

If I may speak so—on the neck
Of a wife's love, takes thence the check
Of conscience, and forbids to doubt
Its measure is to be without
All measure, and a fond excess
Is here her rule of godliness.

I took him not for love but fright;
He did but ask a dreadful right.
In this was love, that he loved me
The first, who was mere poverty.
All that I know of love he taught;
And love is all I know of aught.
My merit is so small by his,
That my demerit is my bliss.
My life is hid with him in Christ,
Never thencefrom to be enticed;
And in his strength have I such rest
As when the baby on my breast
Finds what it knows not how to seek,
And, very happy, very weak,
Lies, only knowing all is well,
Pillow'd on kindness palpable.

II
From Lady Clitheroe To Mary Churchill

Dear Saint, I'm still at High-Hurst Park.
The house is fill'd with folks of mark.

Honoria suits a good estate
Much better than I hoped. How fate
Loads her with happiness and pride!
And such a loving lord, beside!
But between us, Sweet, everything
Has limits, and to build a wing
To this old house, when Courtholm stands
Empty upon his Berkshire lands,
And all that Honor might be near
Papa, was buying love too dear.

With twenty others, there are two
Guests here, whose names will startle you:
Mr. and Mrs. Frederick Graham!
I thought he stay'd away for shame.
He and his wife were ask'd, you know,
And would not come, four years ago.
You recollect Miss Smythe found out
Who she had been, and all about
Her people at the Powder-mill;
And how the fine Aunt tried to instil
Haut ton, and how, at last poor Jane
Had got so shy and gauche that, when
The Dockyard gentry came to sup,
She always had to be lock'd up;
And some one wrote to us and said
Her mother was a kitchen-maid.
Dear Mary, you'll be charm'd to know
It must be all a fib. But, oh,
She is the oddest little Pet
On which my eyes were ever set!
She's so outrée and natural
That, when she first arrived, we all
Wonder'd, as when a robin comes
In through the window to eat crumbs
At breakfast with us. She has sense,
Humility, and confidence;
And, save in dressing just a thought
Gayer in colours than she ought,
(To-day she looks a cross between
Gipsy and Fairy, red and green,)
She always happens to do well.
And yet one never quite can tell
What she might do or utter next.
Lord Clitheroe is much perplex'd.
Her husband, every now and then,
Looks nervous; all the other men
Are charm'd. Yet she has neither grace,
Nor one good feature in her face.
Her eyes, indeed, flame in her head,
Like very altar-fires to Fred,
Whose steps she follows everywhere

Like a tame duck, to the despair
Of Colonel Holmes, who does his part
To break her funny little heart.
Honor's enchanted. 'Tis her view
That people, if they're good and true,
And treated well, and let alone,
Will kindly take to what's their own,
And always be original,
Like children. Honor's just like all
The rest of us! But, thinking so,
'Tis well she miss'd Lord Clitheroe,
Who hates originality,
Though he puts up with it in me.

Poor Mrs. Graham has never been
To the Opera! You should have seen
The innocent way she told the Earl
She thought Plays sinful when a girl,
And now she never had a chance!
Frederick's complacent smile and glance
Towards her, show'd me, past a doubt,
Honoria had been quite cut out.
'Tis very strange; for Mrs. Graham,
Though Frederick's fancy none can blame,
Seems the last woman you'd have thought
Her lover would have ever sought.
She never reads, I find, nor goes
Anywhere; so that I suppose
She got at all she ever knew
By growing up, as kittens do.

Talking of kittens, by-the-bye,
You have more influence than I
With dear Honoria. Get her, Dear,
To be a little more severe
With those sweet Children. They've the run
Of all the place. When school was done,
Maud burst in, while the Earl was there,
With 'Oh, Mama, do be a bear!'

Do you know, Dear, this odd wife of Fred
Adores his old Love in his stead!
She is so nice, yet, I should say,
Not quite the thing for every day.
Wonders are wearying! Felix goes
Next Sunday with her to the Close,
And you will judge.

Honoria asks
All Wiltshire Belles here; Felix basks
Like Puss in fire-shine, when the room
Is thus aflame with female bloom.

But then she smiles when most would pout;
And so his lawless loves go out
With the last brocade. 'Tis not the same,
I fear, with Mrs. Frederick Graham.
Honoria should not have her here,—
And this you might just hint, my Dear,—
For Felix says he never saw
Such proof of what he holds for law,
That 'beauty is love which can be seen.'
Whatever he by this may mean,
Were it not dreadful if he fell
In love with her on principle!

III
From Jane To Mrs. Graham

Mother, I told you how, at first,
I fear'd this visit to the Hurst.
Fred must, I felt, be so distress'd
By aught in me unlike the rest
Who come here. But I find the place
Delightful; there's such ease, and grace,
And kindness, and all seem to be
On such a high equality.
They have not got to think, you know,
How far to make the money go.
But Frederick says it's less the expense
Of money, than of sound good-sense,
Quickness to care what others feel,
And thoughts with nothing to conceal;
Which I'll teach Johnny. Mrs. Vaughan
Was waiting for us on the Lawn,
And kiss'd and call'd me 'Cousin.' Fred
Neglected his old friends, she said.
He laugh'd, and colour'd up at this.
She was, you know, a flame of his;
But I'm not jealous! Luncheon done,
I left him, who had just begun
To talk about the Russian War
With an old Lady, Lady Carr,—
A Countess, but I'm more afraid,
A great deal, of the Lady's Maid,—
And went with Mrs. Vaughan to see
The pictures, which appear'd to be
Of sorts of horses, clowns, and cows
Call'd Wouvermans and Cuyps and Dows.
And then she took me up, to show
Her bedroom, where, long years ago,
A Queen slept. 'Tis all tapestries
Of Cupids, Gods, and Goddesses,
And black, carved oak. A curtain'd door

Leads thence into her soft Boudoir,
Where even her husband may but come
By favour. He, too, has his room,
Kept sacred to his solitude.
Did I not think the plan was good?
She ask'd me; but I said how small
Our house was, and that, after all,
Though Frederick would not say his prayers
At night till I was safe upstairs,
I thought it wrong to be so shy
Of being good when I was by.
'Oh, you should humour him!' she said,
With her sweet voice and smile; and led
The way to where the children ate
Their dinner, and Miss Williams sate.
She's only Nursery-Governess,
Yet they consider her no less
Than Lord or Lady Carr, or me.
Just think how happy she must be!
The Ball-Room, with its painted sky
Where heavy angels seem to fly,
Is a dull place; its size and gloom
Make them prefer, for drawing-room,
The Library, all done up new
And comfortable, with a view
Of Salisbury Spire between the boughs.

When she had shown me through the house,
(I wish I could have let her know
That she herself was half the show;
She is so handsome, and so kind!)
She fetch'd the children, who had dined;
And, taking one in either hand,
Show'd me how all the grounds were plann'd.
The lovely garden gently slopes
To where a curious bridge of ropes
Crosses the Avon to the Park.
We rested by the stream, to mark
The brown backs of the hovering trout.
Frank tickled one, and took it out
From under a stone. We saw his owls,
And awkward Cochin-China fowls,
And shaggy pony in the croft;
And then he dragg'd us to a loft,
Where pigeons, as he push'd the door,
Fann'd clear a breadth of dusty floor,
And set us coughing. I confess
I trembled for my nice silk dress.
I cannot think how Mrs. Vaughan
Ventured with that which she had on,—
A mere white wrapper, with a few
Plain trimmings of a quiet blue,

But, oh, so pretty! Then the bell
For dinner rang. I look'd quite well
('Quite charming,' were the words Fred said,)
With the new gown that I've had made.

I am so proud of Frederick.
He's so high-bred and lordly-like
With Mrs. Vaughan! He's not quite so
At home with me; but that, you know,
I can't expect, or wish. 'Twould hurt,
And seem to mock at my desert.
Not but that I'm a duteous wife
To Fred; but, in another life,
Where all are fair that have been true
I hope I shall be graceful too,
Like Mrs. Vaughan. And, now, good-bye!
That happy thought has made me cry,
And feel half sorry that my cough,
In this fine air, is leaving off.

IV
From Frederick To Mrs. Graham

Honoria, trebly fair and mild
With added loves of lord and child,
Is else unalter'd. Years, which wrong
The rest, touch not her beauty, young
With youth which rather seems her clime,
Than aught that's relative to time.
How beyond hope was heard the prayer
I offer'd in my love's despair!
Could any, whilst there's any woe,
Be wholly blest, then she were so.
She is, and is aware of it,
Her husband's endless benefit;
But, though their daily ways reveal
The depth of private joy they feel,
'Tis not their bearing each to each
That does abroad their secret preach,
But such a lovely good-intent
To all within their government
And friendship as, 'tis well discern'd,
Each of the other must have learn'd;
For no mere dues of neighbourhood
Ever begot so blest a mood.

And fair, indeed, should be the few
God dowers with nothing else to do,
And liberal of their light, and free
To show themselves, that all may see!
For alms let poor men poorly give

The meat whereby men's bodies live;
But they of wealth are stewards wise
Whose graces are their charities.

The sunny charm about this home
Makes all to shine who thither come.
My own dear Jane has caught its grace,
And, honour'd, honours too the place.
Across the lawn I lately walk'd
Alone, and watch'd where mov'd and talk'd,
Gentle and goddess-like of air,
Honoria and some Stranger fair.
I chose a path unblest by these;
When one of the two Goddesses,
With my Wife's voice, but softer, said,
'Will you not walk with us, dear Fred?'

She moves, indeed, the modest peer
Of all the proudest ladies here.
Unawed she talks with men who stand
Among the leaders of the land,
And women beautiful and wise,
With England's greatness in their eyes.
To high, traditional good-sense,
And knowledge ripe without pretence,
And human truth exactly hit
By quiet and conclusive wit,
Listens my little, homely Dove,
Mistakes the points and laughs for love;
And, after, stands and combs her hair,
And calls me much the wittiest there!

With reckless loyalty, dear Wife,
She lays herself about my life!
The joy I might have had of yore
I have not; for 'tis now no more,
With me, the lyric time of youth,
And sweet sensation of the truth.
Yet, past my hope or purpose bless'd,
In my chance choice let be confess'd
The tenderer Providence that rules
The fates of children and of fools!

I kiss'd the kind, warm neck that slept,
And from her side this morning stepp'd,
To bathe my brain from drowsy night
In the sharp air and golden light.
The dew, like frost, was on the pane.
The year begins, though fair, to wane.
There is a fragrance in its breath
Which is not of the flowers, but death;
And green above the ground appear

The lilies of another year.
I wander'd forth, and took my path
Among the bloomless aftermath;
And heard the steadfast robin sing
As if his own warm heart were Spring,
And watch'd him feed where, on the yew,
Hung honey'd drops of crimson dew;
And then return'd, by walls of peach,
And pear-trees bending to my reach,
And rose-beds with the roses gone,
To bright-laid breakfast. Mrs. Vaughan
Was there, none with her. I confess
I love her than of yore no less!
But she alone was loved of old;
Now love is twain, nay, manifold;
For, somehow, he whose daily life
Adjusts itself to one true wife,
Grows to a nuptial, near degree
With all that's fair and womanly.
Therefore, as more than friends, we met,
Without constraint, without regret;
The wedded yoke that each had donn'd
Seeming a sanction, not a bond.

V
From Mrs. Graham

Your love lacks joy, your letter says.
Yes; love requires the focal space
Of recollection or of hope,
Ere it can measure its own scope.
Too soon, too soon comes Death to show
We love more deeply than we know!
The rain, that fell upon the height
Too gently to be call'd delight,
Within the dark vale reappears
As a wild cataract of tears;
And love in life should strive to see
Sometimes what love in death would be!
Easier to love, we so should find,
It is than to be just and kind.

She's gone: shut close the coffin-lid:
What distance for another did
That death has done for her! The good,
Once gazed upon with heedless mood,
Now fills with tears the famish'd eye,
And turns all else to vanity.
'Tis sad to see, with death between,
The good we have pass'd and have not seen!
How strange appear the words of all!

The looks of those that live appal.
They are the ghosts, and check the breath:
There's no reality but death,
And hunger for some signal given
That we shall have our own in heaven.
But this the God of love lets be
A horrible uncertainty.

How great her smallest virtue seems,
How small her greatest fault! Ill dreams
Were those that foil'd with loftier grace
The homely kindness of her face.
'Twas here she sat and work'd, and there
She comb'd and kiss'd the children's hair;
Or, with one baby at her breast,
Another taught, or hush'd to rest.
Praise does the heart no more refuse
To the chief loveliness of use.
Her humblest good is hence most high
In the heavens of fond memory;
And Love says Amen to the word,
A prudent wife is from the Lord.
Her worst gown's kept, ('tis now the best,
As that in which she oftenest dress'd,)
For memory's sake more precious grown
Than she herself was for her own.
Poor child! foolish it seem'd to fly
To sobs instead of dignity,
When she was hurt. Now, more than all,
Heart-rending and angelical
That ignorance of what to do,
Bewilder'd still by wrong from you:
For what man ever yet had grace
Ne'er to abuse his power and place?

No magic of her voice or smile
Suddenly raised a fairy isle,
But fondness for her underwent
An unregarded increment,
Like that which lifts, through centuries,
The coral-reef within the seas,
Till, lo! the land where was the wave,
Alas! 'tis everywhere her grave.

VI
From Jane To Mrs. Graham

Dear Mother, I can surely tell,
Now, that I never shall get well.
Besides the warning in my mind,
All suddenly are grown so kind.

Fred stopp'd the Doctor, yesterday,
Downstairs, and, when he went away,
Came smiling back, and sat with me,
Pale, and conversing cheerfully
About the Spring, and how my cough,
In finer weather, would leave off.
I saw it all, and told him plain
I felt no hope of Spring again.
Then he, after a word of jest,
Burst into tears upon my breast,
And own'd, when he could speak, he knew
There was a little danger, too.
This made me very weak and ill,
And while, last night, I lay quite still,
And, as he fancied, in the deep,
Exhausted rest of my short sleep,
I heard, or dream'd I heard him pray:
'Oh, Father, take her not away!
'Let not life's dear assurance lapse
'Into death's agonised 'Perhaps,'

'A hope without Thy promise, where
'Less than assurance is despair!
'Give me some sign, if go she must,
'That death's not worse than dust to dust,
'Not heaven, on whose oblivious shore
'Joy I may have, but her no more!
'The bitterest cross, it seems to me,
'Of all is infidelity;
'And so, if I may choose, I'll miss
'The kind of heaven which comes to this.
'If doom'd, indeed, this fever ceased,
'To die out wholly, like a beast,
'Forgetting all life's ill success
'In dark and peaceful nothingness,
'I could but say, Thy will be done;
'For, dying thus, I were but one
'Of seed innumerable which ne'er
'In all the worlds shall bloom or bear.
'I've put life past to so poor use
'Well may'st Thou life to come refuse;
'And justice, which the spirit contents,
'Shall still in me all vain laments;
'Nay, pleased, I will, while yet I live,
'Think Thou my forfeit joy may'st give
'To some fresh life, else unelect,
'And heaven not feel my poor defect!
'Only let not Thy method be
'To make that life, and call it me;
'Still less to sever mine in twain,
'And tell each half to live again,
'And count itself the whole! To die,

'Is it love's disintegrity?
'Answer me, 'No,' and I, with grace,
'Will life's brief desolation face,
'My ways, as native to the clime,
'Adjusting to the wintry time,
'Ev'n with a patient cheer thereof—'

He started up, hearing me cough.
Oh, Mother, now my last doubt's gone!
He likes me more than Mrs. Vaughan;
And death, which takes me from his side,
Shows me, in very deed, his bride!

VII
From Jane To Frederick

I leave this, Dear, for you to read,
For strength and hope, when I am dead.
When Grace died, I was so perplex'd,
I could not find one helpful text;
And when, a little while before,
I saw her sobbing on the floor,
Because I told her that in heaven
She would be as the angels even,
And would not want her doll, 'tis true
A horrible fear within me grew,
That, since the preciousness of love
Went thus for nothing, mine might prove
To be no more, and heaven's bliss
Some dreadful good which is not this.

But being about to die makes clear
Many dark things. I have no fear,
Now, that my love, my grief, my joy
Is but a passion for a toy.
I cannot speak at all, I find,
The shining something in my mind,
That shows so much that, if I took
My thoughts all down, 'twould make a book.
God's Word, which lately seem'd above
The simpleness of human love,
To my death-sharpen'd hearing tells
Of little or of nothing else;
And many things I hoped were true,
When first they came, like songs, from you,
Now rise with witness past the reach
Of doubt, and I to you can teach,
As if with felt authority
And as things seen, what you taught me.

Yet how? I have no words but those

Which every one already knows:
As, 'No man hath at any time
'Seen God, but 'tis the love of Him
'Made perfect, and He dwells in us,
'If we each other love.' Or thus,
'My goodness misseth in extent
'Of Thee, Lord! In the excellent
'I know Thee; and the Saints on Earth
'Make all my love and holy mirth.'
And further, 'Inasmuch as ye
'Did it to one of these, to Me
'Ye did it, though ye nothing thought
'Nor knew of Me, in that ye wrought.'

What shall I dread? Will God undo
Our bond, which is all others too?
And when I meet you will you say
To my reclaiming looks, 'Away!
'A dearer love my bosom warms
'With higher rights and holier charms.
'The children, whom thou here may'st see,
'Neighbours that mingle thee and me,
'And gaily on impartial lyres
'Renounce the foolish filial fires
'They felt, with 'Praise to God on high,
''Goodwill to all else equally;'

'The trials, duties, service, tears;
'The many fond, confiding years
'Of nearness sweet with thee apart;
'The joy of body, mind, and heart;
'The love that grew a reckless growth,
'Unmindful that the marriage-oath
'To love in an eternal style
'Meant—only for a little while:
'Sever'd are now those bonds earth-wrought:
'All love, not new, stands here for nought!'

Why, it seems almost wicked, Dear,
Even to utter such a fear!
Are we not 'heirs,' as man and wife,
'Together of eternal life?'
Was Paradise e'er meant to fade,
To make which marriage first was made?
Neither beneath him nor above
Could man in Eden find his Love;
Yet with him in the garden walk'd
His God, and with Him mildly talk'd!
Shall the humble preference offend
In heaven, which God did there commend?
Are 'honourable and undefiled'
The names of aught from heaven exiled?

And are we not forbid to grieve
As without hope? Does God deceive,
And call that hope which is despair,
Namely, the heaven we should not share?
Image and glory of the man,
As he of God, is woman. Can
This holy, sweet proportion die
Into a dull equality?
Are we not one flesh, yea, so far
More than the babe and mother are,
That sons are bid mothers to leave
And to their wives alone to cleave,
'For they two are one flesh?' But 'tis
In the flesh we rise. Our union is,
You know 'tis said, 'great mystery.'
Great mockery, it appears to me;
Poor image of the spousal bond
Of Christ and Church, if loosed beyond
This life!—'Gainst which, and much more yet,
There's not a single word to set.
The speech to the scoffing Sadducee
Is not in point to you and me;
For how could Christ have taught such clods
That Cæsar's things are also God's?
The sort of Wife the Law could make
Might well be 'hated' for Love's sake,
And left, like money, land, or house;
For out of Christ is no true spouse.

I used to think it strange of Him
To make love's after-life so dim,
Or only clear by inference:
But God trusts much to common sense,
And only tells us what, without
His Word, we could not have found out.
On fleshly tables of the heart
He penn'd truth's feeling counterpart
In hopes that come to all: so, Dear,
Trust these, and be of happy cheer,
Nor think that he who has loved well
Is of all men most miserable.

There's much more yet I want to say,
But cannot now. You know my way
Of feeling strong from Twelve till Two
After my wine. I'll write to you
Daily some words, which you shall have
To break the silence of the grave.

VIII
From Jane To Frederick

You think, perhaps, 'Ah, could she know
How much I loved her!' Dear, I do!
And you may say, 'Of this new awe
'Of heart which makes her fancies law,
'These watchful duties of despair,
'She does not dream, she cannot care!'
Frederick, you see how false that is,
Or how could I have written this?
And, should it ever cross your mind
That, now and then, you were unkind,
You never, never were at all!
Remember that! It's natural
For one like Mr. Vaughan to come,
From a morning's useful pastime, home,
And greet, with such a courteous zest,
His handsome wife, still newly dress'd,
As if the Bird of Paradise
Should daily change her plumage thrice.
He's always well, she's always gay.
Of course! But he who toils all day,
And comes home hungry, tired, or cold,
And feels 'twould do him good to scold
His wife a little, let him trust
Her love, and say the things he must,
Till sooth'd in mind by meat and rest.
If, after that, she's well caress'd,
And told how good she is, to bear
His humour, fortune makes it fair.
Women like men to be like men;
That is, at least, just now and then.
Thus, I have nothing to forgive,
But those first years, (how could I live!)
When, though I really did behave
So stupidly, you never gave
One unkind word or look at all:
As if I was some animal
You pitied! Now, in later life,
You used me like a proper Wife.

You feel, Dear, in your present mood,
Your Jane, since she was kind and good,
A child of God, a living soul,
Was not so different, on the whole,
From Her who had a little more
Of God's best gifts: but, oh, be sure,
My dear, dear Love, to take no blame
Because you could not feel the same
Towards me, living, as when dead.
A hungry man must needs think bread
So sweet! and, only at their rise
And setting, blessings, to the eyes,

Like the sun's course, grow visible.
If you are sad, remember well,
Against delusions of despair,
That memory sees things as they were,
And not as they were misenjoy'd,
And would be still, if ought destroy'd
The glory of their hopelessness:
So that, in truth, you had me less
In days when necessary zeal
For my perfection made you feel
My faults the most, than now your love
Forgets but where it can approve.
You gain by loss, if that seem'd small
Possess'd, which, being gone, turns all
Surviving good to vanity.
Oh, Fred, this makes it sweet to die!

Say to yourself: "Tis comfort yet
'I made her that which I regret;
'And parting might have come to pass
'In a worse season; as it was,
'Love an eternal temper took,
'Dipp'd, glowing, in Death's icy brook!'
Or say, 'On her poor feeble head
'This might have fallen: 'tis mine instead!
'And so great evil sets me free
'Henceforward from calamity.
'And, in her little children, too,
'How much for her I yet can do!'
And grieve not for these orphans even;
For central to the love of Heaven
Is each child as each star to space.
This truth my dying love has grace
To trust with a so sure content,
I fear I seem indifferent.

You must not think a child's small heart
Cold, because it and grief soon part.
Fanny will keep them all away,
Lest you should hear them laugh and play,
Before the funeral's over. Then
I hope you'll be yourself again,
And glad, with all your soul, to find
How God thus to the sharpest wind
Suits the shorn lambs. Instruct them, Dear,
For my sake, in His love and fear.
And show how, till their journey's done,
Not to be weary they must run.

Strive not to dissipate your grief
By any lightness. True relief
Of sorrow is by sorrow brought.

And yet for sorrow's sake, you ought
To grieve with measure. Do not spend
So good a power to no good end!
Would you, indeed, have memory stay
In the heart, lock up and put away
Relics and likenesses and all
Musings, which waste what they recall.
True comfort, and the only thing
To soothe without diminishing
A prized regret, is to match here,
By a strict life, God's love severe.
Yet, after all, by nature's course,
Feeling must lose its edge and force.
Again you'll reach the desert tracts
Where only sin or duty acts.
But, if love always lit our path,
Where were the trial of our faith?

Oh, should the mournful honeymoon
Of death be over strangely soon,
And life-long resolutions, made
In grievous haste, as quickly fade,
Seeming the truth of grief to mock,
Think, Dearest, 'tis not by the clock
That sorrow goes! A month of tears
Is more than many, many years
Of common time. Shun, if you can,
However, any passionate plan.
Grieve with the heart; let not the head
Grieve on, when grief of heart is dead;
For all the powers of life defy
A superstitious constancy.

The only bond I hold you to
Is that which nothing can undo.
A man is not a young man twice;
And if, of his young years, he lies
A faithful score in one wife's breast,
She need not mind who has the rest.
In this do what you will, dear Love,
And feel quite sure that I approve.
And, should it chance as it may be,
Give her my wedding-ring from me;
And never dream that you can err
T'wards me by being good to her;
Nor let remorseful thoughts destroy
In you the kindly flowering joy
And pleasure of the natural life.

But don't forget your fond, dead Wife.
And, Frederick, should you ever be
Tempted to think your love of me

All fancy, since it drew its breath
So much more sweetly after death,
Remember that I never did
A single thing you once forbid;
All poor folk liked me; and, at the end,
Your Cousin call'd me 'Dearest Friend!'

And, now, 'twill calm your grief to know,—
You, who once loved Honoria so,—
There's kindness, that's look'd kindly on,
Between her Emily and John.
Thus, in your children, you will wed!
And John seems so much comforted,
(Like Isaac when his mother died
And fair Rebekah was his bride),
By his new hope, for losing me!
So all is happiness, you see.
And that reminds me how, last night,
I dreamt of heaven, with great delight.
A strange, kind Lady watch'd my face,
Kiss'd me, and cried, 'His hope found grace!'
She bade me then, in the crystal floor,
Look at myself, myself no more;
And bright within the mirror shone
Honoria's smile, and yet my own!
'And, when you talk, I hear,' she sigh'd,
'How much he loved her! Many a bride
'In heaven such countersemblance wears
'Through what Love deem'd rejected prayers.'
She would have spoken still; but, lo,
One of a glorious troop, aglow
From some great work, towards her came,
And she so laugh'd, 'twas such a flame,
Aaron's twelve jewels seem'd to mix
With the lights of the Seven Candlesticks.

IX
From Lady Clitheroe To Mrs. Graham

My dearest Aunt, the Wedding-day,
But for Jane's loss, and you away,
Was all a Bride from heaven could beg!
Skies bluer than the sparrow's egg,
And clearer than the cuckoo's call;
And such a sun! the flowers all
With double ardour seem'd to blow!
The very daisies were a show,
Expanded with uncommon pride,
Like little pictures of the Bride.

Your Great-Niece and your Grandson were

Perfection of a pretty pair.
How well Honoria's girls turn out,
Although they never go about!
Dear me, what trouble and expense
It took to teach mine confidence!
Hers greet mankind as I've heard say
That wild things do, where beasts of prey
Were never known, nor any men
Have met their fearless eyes till then.
Their grave, inquiring trust to find
All creatures of their simple kind
Quite disconcerts bold coxcombry,
And makes less perfect candour shy.
Ah, Mrs. Graham! people may scoff,
But how your home-kept girls go off!
How Hymen hastens to unband
The waist that ne'er felt waltzer's hand!
At last I see my Sister's right,
And I've told Maud this very night,
(But, oh, my daughters have such wills!)
To knit, and only dance quadrilles.

You say Fred never writes to you
Frankly, as once he used to do,
About himself; and you complain
He shared with none his grief for Jane.
It all comes of the foolish fright
Men feel at the word, hypocrite.
Although, when first in love, sometimes
They rave in letters, talk, and rhymes,
When once they find, as find they must,
How hard 'tis to be hourly just
To those they love, they are dumb for shame,
Where we, you see, talk on the same.

Honoria, to whose heart alone
He seems to open all his own,
At times has tears in her kind eyes,
After their private colloquies.
He's her most favour'd guest, and moves
My spleen by his impartial loves.
His pleasure has some inner spring
Depending not on anything.
Petting our Polly, none e'er smiled
More fondly on his favourite child;
Yet, playing with his own, it is
Somehow as if it were not his.
He means to go again to sea,
Now that the wedding's over. He
Will leave to Emily and John
The little ones to practise on;
And Major-domo, Mrs. Rouse,

A deal old soul from Wilton House,
Will scold the housemaids and the cook,
Till Emily has learn'd to look
A little braver than a lamb
Surprised by dogs without its dam!

Do, dear Aunt, use your influence,
And try to teach some plain good sense
To Mary. 'Tis not yet too late
To make her change her chosen state
Of single silliness. In truth,
I fancy that, with fading youth,
Her will now wavers. Yesterday,
Though, till the Bride was gone away,
Joy shone from Mary's loving heart,
I found her afterwards apart,
Hysterically sobbing. I
Knew much too well to ask her why.
This marrying of Nieces daunts
The bravest souls of maiden Aunts.
Though Sisters' children often blend
Sweetly the bonds of child and friend,
They are but reeds to rest upon.
When Emily comes back with John,
Her right to go downstairs before
Aunt Mary will but be the more
Observed if kindly waived, and how
Shall these be as they were, when now
Niece has her John, and Aunt the sense
Of her superior innocence?
Somehow, all loves, however fond,
Prove lieges of the nuptial bond;
And she who dares at this to scoff,
Finds all the rest in time drop off;
While marriage, like a mushroom-ring,
Spreads its sure circle every Spring.

She twice refused George Vane, you know;
Yet, when he died three years ago
In the Indian war, she put on gray,
And wears no colours to this day.
And she it is who charges me,
Dear Aunt, with 'inconsistency!'

X
From Frederick To Honoria

Cousin, my thoughts no longer try
To cast the fashion of the sky.
Imagination can extend
Scarcely in part to comprehend

The sweetness of our common food
Ambrosial, which ingratitude
And impious inadvertence waste,
Studious to eat but not to taste.
And who can tell what's yet in store
There, but that earthly things have more
Of all that makes their inmost bliss,
And life's an image still of this,
But haply such a glorious one
As is the rainbow of the sun?
Sweet are your words, but, after all
Their mere reversal may befall
The partners of His glories who
Daily is crucified anew:
Splendid privations, martyrdoms
To which no weak remission comes,
Perpetual passion for the good
Of them that feel no gratitude,
Far circlings, as of planets' fires,
Round never-to-be-reach'd desires,
Whatever rapturously sighs
That life is love, love sacrifice.
All I am sure of heaven is this:
Howe'er the mode, I shall not miss
One true delight which I have known.
Not on the changeful earth alone
Shall loyalty remain unmoved
T'wards everything I ever loved.
So Heaven's voice calls, like Rachel's voice
To Jacob in the field, 'Rejoice!
'Serve on some seven more sordid years,
'Too short for weariness or tears;
'Serve on; then, oh, Beloved, well-tried,
'Take me for ever as thy Bride!'

XI
From Mary Churchill To The Dean

Charles does me honour, but 'twere vain
To reconsider now again,
And so to doubt the clear-shown truth
I sought for, and received, when youth,
Being fair, and woo'd by one whose love
Was lovely, fail'd my mind to move.
God bids them by their own will go,
Who ask again the things they know!
I grieve for my infirmity,
And ignorance of how to be
Faithful, at once, to the heavenly life,
And the fond duties of a wife.
Narrow am I and want the art

To love two things with all my heart.
Occupied singly in His search,
Who, in the Mysteries of the Church,
Returns, and calls them Clouds of Heaven,
I tread a road, straight, hard, and even;
But fear to wander all confused,
By two-fold fealty abused.
Either should I the one forget,
Or scantly pay the other's debt.

You bid me, Father, count the cost.
I have; and all that must be lost
I feel as only woman can.
To make the heart's wealth of some man,
And through the untender world to move,
Wrapt safe in his superior love,
How sweet! How sweet the household round
Of duties, and their narrow bound,
So plain, that to transgress were hard,
Yet full of manifest reward!
The charities not marr'd, like mine,
With chance of thwarting laws divine;
The world's regards and just delight
In one that's clearly, kindly right,
How sweet! Dear Father, I endure,
Not without sharp regret, be sure,
To give up such glad certainty,
For what, perhaps, may never be.
For nothing of my state I know,
But that t'ward heaven I seem to go,
As one who fondly landward hies
Along a deck that seaward flies.
With every year, meantime, some grace
Of earthly happiness gives place
To humbling ills, the very charms
Of youth being counted, henceforth, harms:
To blush already seems absurd;
Nor know I whether I should herd
With girls or wives, or sadlier balk
Maids' merriment or matrons' talk.

But strait's the gate of life! O'er late,
Besides, 'twere now to change my fate:
For flowers and fruit of love to form,
It must be Spring as well as warm.
The world's delight my soul dejects,
Revenging all my disrespects
Of old, with incapacity
To chime with even its harmless glee,
Which sounds, from fields beyond my range,
Like fairies' music, thin and strange.
With something like remorse, I grant

The world has beauty which I want;
And if, instead of judging it,
I at its Council chance to sit,
Or at its gay and order'd Feast,
My place seems lower than the least.
The conscience of the life to be
Smites me with inefficiency,
And makes me all unfit to bless
With comfortable earthliness
The rest-desiring brain of man.
Finally, then, I fix my plan
To dwell with Him that dwells apart
In the highest heaven and lowliest heart;
Nor will I, to my utter loss,
Look to pluck roses from the Cross.
As for the good of human love,
'Twere countercheck almost enough
To think that one must die before
The other; and perhaps 'tis more
In love's last interest to do
Nought the least contrary thereto,
Than to be blest, and be unjust,
Or suffer injustice; as they must,
Without a miracle, whose pact
Compels to mutual life and act,
Whether love shines, or darkness sleeps
Cold on the spirit's changeful deeps.

Enough if, to my earthly share,
Fall gleams that keep me from despair.
Happy the things we here discern;
More happy those for which we yearn;
But measurelessly happy above
All else are those we guess not of!

XII
From Felix To Honoria

Dearest, my Love and Wife, 'tis long
Ago I closed the unfinish'd song
Which never could be finish'd; nor
Will ever Poet utter more
Of love than I did, watching well
To lure to speech the unspeakable!
'Why, having won her, do I woo?'
That final strain to the last height flew
Of written joy, which wants the smile
And voice that are, indeed, the while
They last, the very things you speak,
Honoria, who mak'st music weak
With ways that say, 'Shall I not be

'As kind to all as Heaven to me?'
And yet, ah, twenty-fold my Bride!
Rising, this twentieth festal-tide,
You still soft sleeping, on this day
Of days, some words I long to say,
Some words superfluously sweet
Of fresh assurance, thus to greet
Your waking eyes, which never grow
Weary of telling what I know
So well, yet only well enough
To wish for further news thereof.

Here, in this early autumn dawn,
By windows opening on the lawn,
Where sunshine seems asleep, though bright,
And shadows yet are sharp with night,
And, further on, the wealthy wheat
Bends in a golden drowse, how sweet
To sit and cast my careless looks
Around my walls of well-read books,
Wherein is all that stands redeem'd
From time's huge wreck, all men have dream'd
Of truth, and all by poets known
Of feeling, and in weak sort shown,
And, turning to my heart again,
To find I have what makes them vain,
The thanksgiving mind, which wisdom sums,
And you, whereby it freshly comes
As on that morning, (can there be
Twenty-two years 'twixt it and me?)
When, thrill'd with hopeful love I rose
And came in haste to Sarum Close,
Past many a homestead slumbering white
In lonely and pathetic light,
Merely to fancy which drawn blind
Of thirteen had my Love behind,
And in her sacred neighbourhood
To feel that sweet scorn of all good
But her, which let the wise forfend
When wisdom learns to comprehend!

Dearest, as each returning May
I see the season new and gay
With new joy and astonishment,
And Nature's infinite ostent
Of lovely flowers in wood and mead,
That weet not whether any heed,
So see I, daily wondering, you,
And worship with a passion new
The Heaven that visibly allows
Its grace to go about my house,
The partial Heaven, that, though I err

And mortal am, gave all to her
Who gave herself to me. Yet I
Boldly thank Heaven, (and so defy
The beggarly soul'd humbleness
Which fears God's bounty to confess,)
That I was fashion'd with a mind
Seeming for this great gift design'd,
So naturally it moved above
All sordid contraries of love,
Strengthen'd in youth with discipline
Of light, to follow the divine
Vision, (which ever to the dark
Is such a plague as was the ark
In Ashdod, Gath, and Ekron,) still
Discerning with the docile will
Which comes of full persuaded thought,
That intimacy in love is nought
Without pure reverence, whereas this,
In tearfullest banishment, is bliss.

And so, dearest Honoria, I
Have never learn'd the weary sigh
Of those that to their love-feasts went,
Fed, and forgot the Sacrament;
And not a trifle now occurs
But sweet initiation stirs
Of new-discover'd joy, and lends
To feeling change that never ends;
And duties, which the many irk,
Are made all wages and no work.

How sing of such things save to her,
Love's self, so love's interpreter?
How the supreme rewards confess
Which crown the austere voluptuousness
Of heart, that earns, in midst of wealth,
The appetite of want and health,
Relinquishes the pomp of life
And beauty to the pleasant Wife
At home, and does all joy despise
As out of place but in her eyes?
How praise the years and gravity
That make each favour seem to be
A lovelier weakness for her lord?
And, ah, how find the tender word
To tell aright of love that glows
The fairer for the fading rose?
Of frailty which can weight the arm
To lean with thrice its girlish charm?
Of grace which, like this autumn day,
Is not the sad one of decay,
Yet one whose pale brow pondereth

The far-off majesty of death?
How tell the crowd, whom passion rends,
That love grows mild as it ascends?
That joy's most high and distant mood
Is lost, not found in dancing blood;
Albeit kind acts and smiling eyes,
And all those fond realities
Which are love's words, in us mean more
Delight than twenty years before?

How, Dearest, finish, without wrong
To the speechless heart, the unfinish'd song,
Its high, eventful passages
Consisting, say, of things like these:—

One morning, contrary to law,
Which, for the most, we held in awe,
Commanding either not to intrude
On the other's place of solitude
Or solitary mind, for fear
Of coming there when God was near,
And finding so what should be known
To Him who is merciful alone,
And views the working ferment base
Of waking flesh and sleeping grace,
Not as we view, our kindness check'd
By likeness of our own defect,
I, venturing to her room, because
(Mark the excuse!) my Birthday 'twas,
Saw, here across a careless chair,
A ball-dress flung, as light as air,
And, here, beside a silken couch,
Pillows which did the pressure vouch
Of pious knees, (sweet piety!
Of goodness made and charity,
If gay looks told the heart's glad sense,
Much rather than of penitence,)
And, on the couch, an open book,
And written list—I did not look,
Yet just in her clear writing caught:—
'Habitual faults of life and thought
'Which most I need deliverance from.'
I turn'd aside, and saw her come
Adown the filbert-shaded way,
Beautified with her usual gay
Hypocrisy of perfectness,
Which made her heart, and mine no less,
So happy! And she cried to me,
'You lose by breaking rules, you see!
'Your Birthday treat is now half-gone
'Of seeing my new ball-dress on.'
And, meeting so my lovely Wife,

A passing pang, to think that life
Was mortal, when I saw her laugh,
Shaped in my mind this epitaph:
'Faults had she, child of Adam's stem,
'But only Heaven knew of them.'

Or thus:

For many a dreadful day,
In sea-side lodgings sick she lay,
Noteless of love, nor seem'd to hear
The sea, on one side, thundering near,
Nor, on the other, the loud Ball
Held nightly in the public hall;
Nor vex'd they my short slumbers, though
I woke up if she breathed too low.
Thus, for three months, with terrors rife,
The pending of her precious life
I watch'd o'er; and the danger, at last,
The kind Physician said, was past.
Howbeit, for seven harsh weeks the East
Breathed witheringly, and Spring's growth ceased,
And so she only did not die;
Until the bright and blighting sky
Changed into cloud, and the sick flowers
Remember'd their perfumes, and showers
Of warm, small rain refreshing flew
Before the South, and the Park grew,
In three nights, thick with green. Then she
Revived, no less than flower and tree,
In the mild air, and, the fourth day,
Look'd supernaturally gay
With large, thanksgiving eyes, that shone,
The while I tied her bonnet on,
So that I led her to the glass,
And bade her see how fair she was,
And how love visibly could shine.
Profuse of hers, desiring mine,
And mindful I had loved her most
When beauty seem'd a vanish'd boast,
She laugh'd. I press'd her then to me,
Nothing but soft humility;
Nor e'er enhanced she with such charms
Her acquiescence in my arms.
And, by her sweet love-weakness made
Courageous, powerful, and glad,
In a clear illustration high
Of heavenly affection, I
Perceived that utter love is all
The same as to be rational,
And that the mind and heart of love,
Which think they cannot do enough,

Are truly the everlasting doors
Wherethrough, all unpetition'd, pours
The eternal pleasance. Wherefore we
Had innermost tranquillity,
And breathed one life with such a sense
Of friendship and of confidence,
That, recollecting the sure word:
'If two of you are in accord,
'On earth, as touching any boon
'Which ye shall ask, it shall be done
'In heaven,' we ask'd that heaven's bliss
Might ne'er be any less than this;
And, for that hour, we seem'd to have
The secret of the joy we gave.

How sing of such things, save to her,
Love's self, so love's interpreter?
How read from such a homely page
In the ear of this unhomely age?
'Tis now as when the Prophet cried:
'The nation hast Thou multiplied,
'But Thou hast not increased the joy!'
And yet, ere wrath or rot destroy
Of England's state the ruin fair,
Oh, might I so its charm declare,
That, in new Lands, in far-off years,
Delighted he should cry that hears:
'Great is the Land that somewhat best
'Works, to the wonder of the rest!
'We, in our day, have better done
'This thing or that than any one;
'And who but, still admiring, sees
'How excellent for images
'Was Greece, for laws how wise was Rome;
'But read this Poet, and say if home
'And private love did e'er so smile
'As in that ancient English isle!'

XIII
From Lady Clitheroe To Emily Graham

My dearest Niece, I'm charm'd to hear
The scenery's fine at Windermere,
And glad a six-weeks' wife defers
In the least to wisdom not yet hers.
But, Child, I've no advice to give!
Rules only make it hard to live.
And where's the good of having been
Well taught from seven to seventeen,
If, married, you may not leave off,
And say, at last, 'I'm good enough!'

Weeding out folly, still leave some.
It gives both lightness and aplomb.
We know, however wise by rule,
Woman is still by nature fool;
And men have sense to like her all
The more when she is natural.
'Tis true that, if we choose, we can
Mock to a miracle the man;
But iron in the fire red hot,
Though 'tis the heat, the fire 'tis not:
And who, for such a feint, would pledge
The babe's and woman's privilege,
No duties and a thousand rights?
Besides, defect love's flow incites,
As water in a well will run
Only the while 'tis drawn upon.

'Point de culte sans mystère,' you say,
'And what if that should die away?'
Child, never fear that either could
Pull from Saint Cupid's face the hood.
The follies natural to each
Surpass the other's moral reach.
Just think how men, with sword and gun,
Will really fight, and never run;
And all in sport: they would have died,
For sixpence more, on the other side!
A woman's heart must ever warm
At such odd ways: and so we charm
By strangeness which, the more they mark,
The more men get into the dark.
The marvel, by familiar life,
Grows, and attaches to the wife
By whom it grows. Thus, silly Girl,
To John you'll always be the pearl
In the oyster of the universe;
And, though in time he'll treat you worse,
He'll love you more, you need not doubt,
And never, never find you out!

My Dear, I know that dreadful thought
That you've been kinder than you ought.
It almost makes you hate him! Yet
'Tis wonderful how men forget,
And how a merciful Providence
Deprives our husbands of all sense
Of kindness past, and makes them deem
We always were what now we seem.
For their own good we must, you know,
However plain the way we go,
Still make it strange with stratagem;
And instinct tells us that, to them,

'Tis always right to bate their price.
Yet I must say they're rather nice,
And, oh, so easily taken in
To cheat them almost seems a sin!
And, Dearest, 'twould be most unfair
To John your feelings to compare
With his, or any man's; for she
Who loves at all loves always; he,
Who loves far more, loves yet by fits,
And when the wayward wind remits
To blow, his feelings faint and drop
Like forge-flames when the bellows stop.
Such things don't trouble you at all
When once you know they're natural.

My love to John; and, pray, my Dear,
Don't let me see you for a year;
Unless, indeed, ere then you've learn'd
That Beauties wed are blossoms turn'd
To unripe codlings, meant to dwell
In modest shadow hidden well,
Till this green stage again permute
To glow of flowers with good of fruit.
I will not have my patience tried
By your absurd new-married pride,
That scorns the world's slow-gather'd sense,
Ties up the hands of Providence,
Rules babes, before there's hope of one,
Better than mothers e'er have done,
And, for your poor particular,
Neglects delights and graces far
Beyond your crude and thin conceit.
Age has romance almost as sweet
And much more generous than this
Of yours and John's. With all the bliss
Of the evenings when you coo'd with him,
And upset home for your sole whim,
You might have envied, were you wise,
The tears within your Mother's eyes,
Which, I dare say, you did not see.
But let that pass! Yours yet will be,
I hope, as happy, kind, and true
As lives which now seem void to you.
Have you not seen shop-painters paste
Their gold in sheets, then rub to waste
Full half, and, lo, you read the name?
Well, Time, my Dear, does much the same
With this unmeaning glare of love.

But, though you yet may much improve,
In marriage, be it still confess'd,
There's little merit at the best.

Some half-a-dozen lives, indeed,
Which else would not have had the need,
Get food and nurture, as the price
Of antedated Paradise;
But what's that to the varied want
Succour'd by Mary, your dear Aunt,
Who put the bridal crown thrice by,
For that of which virginity,
So used, has hope? She sends her love,
As usual with a proof thereof—
Papa's discourse, which you, no doubt,
Heard none of, neatly copied out
Whilst we were dancing. All are well,
Adieu, for there's the Luncheon Bell.

The Wedding Sermon

I
The truths of Love are like the sea
For clearness and for mystery.
Of that sweet love which, startling, wakes
Maiden and Youth, and mostly breaks
The word of promise to the ear,
But keeps it, after many a year,
To the full spirit, how shall I speak?
My memory with age is weak,
And I for hopes do oft suspect
The things I seem to recollect.
Yet who but must remember well
'Twas this made heaven intelligible
As motive, though 'twas small the power
The heart might have, for even an hour,
To hold possession of the height
Of nameless pathos and delight!

II
In Godhead rise, thither flow back
All loves, which, as they keep or lack,
In their return, the course assign'd,
Are virtue or sin. Love's every kind,
Lofty or low, of spirit or sense,
Desire is, or benevolence.
He who is fairer, better, higher
Than all His works, claims all desire,
And in His Poor, His Proxies, asks
Our whole benevolence: He tasks,
Howbeit, His People by their powers;
And if, my Children, you, for hours,
Daily, untortur'd in the heart,
Can worship, and time's other part

Give, without rough recoils of sense,
To the claims ingrate of indigence,
Happy are you, and fit to be
Wrought to rare heights of sanctity,
For the humble to grow humbler at.
But if the flying spirit falls flat,
After the modest spell of prayer
That saves the day from sin and care,
And the upward eye a void descries,
And praises are hypocrisies,
And, in the soul, o'erstrain'd for grace,
A godless anguish grows apace;
Or, if impartial charity
Seems, in the act, a sordid lie,
Do not infer you cannot please
God, or that He His promises
Postpones, but be content to love
No more than He accounts enough.
Account them poor enough who want
Any good thing which you can grant;
And fathom well the depths of life
In loves of Husband and of Wife,
Child, Mother, Father; simple keys
To what cold faith calls mysteries.

III
The love of marriage claims, above
All other kinds, the name of love,
As perfectest, though not so high
As love which Heaven with single eye
Considers. Equal and entire,
Therein benevolence, desire,
Elsewhere ill-join'd or found apart,
Become the pulses of one heart,
Which now contracts, and now dilates,
And, both to the height exalting, mates
Self-seeking to self-sacrifice.
Nay, in its subtle paradise
(When purest) this one love unites
All modes of these two opposites,
All balanced in accord so rich
Who may determine which is which?
Chiefly God's Love does in it live,
And nowhere else so sensitive;
For each is all that the other's eye,
In the vague vast of Deity,
Can comprehend and so contain
As still to touch and ne'er to strain
The fragile nerves of joy. And then
'Tis such a wise goodwill to men
And politic economy
As in a prosperous State we see,

Where every plot of common land
Is yielded to some private hand
To fence about and cultivate.
Does narrowness its praise abate?
Nay, the infinite of man is found
But in the beating of its bound,
And, if a brook its banks o'erpass,
'Tis not a sea, but a morass.

IV

No giddiest hope, no wildest guess
Of Love's most innocent loftiness
Had dared to dream of its own worth,
Till Heaven's bold sun-gleam lit the earth.
Christ's marriage with the Church is more,
My Children, than a metaphor.
The heaven of heavens is symbol'd where
The torch of Psyche flash'd despair.

But here I speak of heights, and heights
Are hardly scaled. The best delights
Of even this homeliest passion, are
In the most perfect souls so rare,
That they who feel them are as men
Sailing the Southern ocean, when,
At midnight, they look up, and eye
The starry Cross, and a strange sky
Of brighter stars; and sad thoughts come
To each how far he is from home.

V

Love's inmost nuptial sweetness see
In the doctrine of virginity!
Could lovers, at their dear wish, blend,
'Twould kill the bliss which they intend;
For joy is love's obedience
Against the law of natural sense;
And those perpetual yearnings sweet
Of lives which dream that they can meet
Are given that lovers never may
Be without sacrifice to lay
On the high altar of true love,
With tears of vestal joy. To move
Frantic, like comets to our bliss,
Forgetting that we always miss,
And so to seek and fly the sun,
By turns, around which love should run,
Perverts the ineffable delight
Of service guerdon'd with full sight
And pathos of a hopeless want,
To an unreal victory's vaunt,
And plaint of an unreal defeat.

Yet no less dangerous misconceit
May also be of the virgin will,
Whose goal is nuptial blessing still,
And whose true being doth subsist,
There where the outward forms are miss'd,
In those who learn and keep the sense
Divine of 'due benevolence,'
Seeking for aye, without alloy
Of selfish thought, another's joy,
And finding in degrees unknown
That which in act they shunn'd, their own.
For all delights of earthly love
Are shadows of the heavens, and move
As other shadows do; they flee
From him that follows them; and he
Who flies, for ever finds his feet
Embraced by their pursuings sweet.

VI
Then, even in love humane, do I
Not counsel aspirations high,
So much as sweet and regular
Use of the good in which we are.
As when a man along the ways
Walks, and a sudden music plays,
His step unchanged, he steps in time,
So let your Grace with Nature chime.
Her primal forces burst, like straws,
The bonds of uncongenial laws.
Right life is glad as well as just,
And, rooted strong in 'This I must,'
It bears aloft the blossom gay
And zephyr-toss'd, of 'This I may;'
Whereby the complex heavens rejoice
In fruits of uncommanded choice.
Be this your rule: seeking delight,
Esteem success the test of right;
For 'gainst God's will much may be done,
But nought enjoy'd, and pleasures none
Exist, but, like to springs of steel,
Active no longer than they feel
The checks that make them serve the soul,
They take their vigour from control.
A man need only keep but well
The Church's indispensable
First precepts, and she then allows,
Nay, more, she bids him, for his spouse,
Leave even his heavenly Father's awe,
At times, and His immaculate law,
Construed in its extremer sense.
Jehovah's mild magnipotence
Smiles to behold His children play

In their own free and childish way,
And can His fullest praise descry
In the exuberant liberty
Of those who, having understood
The glory of the Central Good,
And how souls ne'er may match or merge,
But as they thitherward converge,
Take in love's innocent gladness part
With infantine, untroubled heart,
And faith that, straight t'wards heaven's far Spring,
Sleeps, like the swallow, on the wing.

VII

Lovers, once married, deem their bond
Then perfect, scanning nought beyond
For love to do but to sustain
The spousal hour's delighted gain.
But time and a right life alone
Fulfil the promise then foreshown.
The Bridegroom and the Bride withal
Are but unwrought material
Of marriage; nay, so far is love,
Thus crown'd, from being thereto enough,
Without the long, compulsive awe
Of duty, that the bond of law
Does oftener marriage-love evoke,
Than love, which does not wear the yoke
Of legal vows, submits to be
Self-rein'd from ruinous liberty.
Lovely is love; but age well knows
'Twas law which kept the lover's vows
Inviolate through the year or years
Of worship pieced with panic fears,
When she who lay within his breast
Seem'd of all women perhaps the best,
But not the whole, of womankind,
Or love, in his yet wayward mind,
Had ghastly doubts its precious life
Was pledged for aye to the wrong wife.

Could it be else? A youth pursues
A maid, whom chance, not he, did choose,
Till to his strange arms hurries she
In a despair of modesty.
Then, simply and without pretence
Of insight or experience,
They plight their vows. The parents say
'We cannot speak them yea or nay;
'The thing proceedeth from the Lord!'
And wisdom still approves their word;
For God created so these two
They match as well as others do

That take more pains, and trust Him less
Who never fails, if ask'd, to bless
His children's helpless ignorance
And blind election of life's chance.
Verily, choice not matters much,
If but the woman's truly such,
And the young man has led the life
Without which how shall e'er the wife
Be the one woman in the world?
Love's sensitive tendrils sicken, curl'd
Round folly's former stay; for 'tis
The doom of all unsanction'd bliss
To mock some good that, gain'd, keeps still
The taint of the rejected ill.

VIII
Howbeit, though both were perfect, she
Of whom the maid was prophecy
As yet lives not, and Love rebels
Against the law of any else;
And, as a steed takes blind alarm,
Disowns the rein, and hunts his harm,
So, misdespairing word and act
May now perturb the happiest pact.

The more, indeed, is love, the more
Peril to love is now in store.
Against it nothing can be done
But only this: leave ill alone!
Who tries to mend his wife succeeds
As he who knows not what he needs.
He much affronts a worth as high
As his, and that equality
Of spirits in which abide the grace
And joy of her subjected place;
And does the still growth check and blurr
Of contraries, confusing her
Who better knows what he desires
Than he, and to that mark aspires
With perfect zeal, and a deep wit
Which nothing helps but trusting it.

So, loyally o'erlooking all
In which love's promise short may fall
Of full performance, honour that
As won, which aye love worketh at!
It is but as the pedigree
Of perfectness which is to be
That our best good can honour claim;
Yet honour to deny were shame
And robbery; for it is the mould
Wherein to beauty runs the gold

Of good intention, and the prop
That lifts to the sun the earth-drawn crop
Of human sensibilities.

Such honour, with a conduct wise
In common things, as, not to steep
The lofty mind of love in sleep
Of over much familiarness;
Not to degrade its kind caress,
As those do that can feel no more,
So give themselves to pleasures o'er;
Not to let morning-sloth destroy
The evening-flower, domestic joy;
Not by uxoriousness to chill
The warm devotion of her will
Who can but half her love confer
On him that cares for nought but her;—

These, and like obvious prudences
Observed, he's safest that relies,
For the hope she will not always seem,
Caught, but a laurel or a stream,
On time; on her unsearchable
Love-wisdom; on their work done well,
Discreet with mutual aid; on might
Of shared affliction and delight;
On pleasures that so childish be
They're 'shamed to let the children see,
By which life keeps the valleys low
Where love does naturally grow;
On much whereof hearts have account,
Though heads forget; on babes, chief fount
Of union, and for which babes are
No less than this for them, nay far
More, for the bond of man and wife
To the very verge of future life
Strengthens, and yearns for brighter day,
While others, with their use, decay;
And, though true marriage purpose keeps
Of offspring, as the centre sleeps
Within the wheel, transmitting thence
Fury to the circumference,
Love's self the noblest offspring is,
And sanction of the nuptial kiss;
Lastly, on either's primal curse,
Which help and sympathy reverse
To blessings.

IX
God, who may be well
Jealous of His chief miracle,
Bids sleep the meddling soul of man,

Through the long process of this plan,
Whereby, from his unweeting side,
The Wife's created, and the Bride,
That chance one of her strange, sweet sex
He to his glad life did annex,
Grows more and more, by day and night,
The one in the whole world opposite
Of him, and in her nature all
So suited and reciprocal
To his especial form of sense,
Affection, and intelligence,
That, whereas love at first had strange
Relapses into lust of change,
It now finds (wondrous this, but true!)
The long-accustom'd only new,
And the untried common; and, whereas
An equal seeming danger was
Of likeness lacking joy and force,
Or difference reaching to divorce,
Now can the finish'd lover see
Marvel of me most far from me,
Whom without pride he may admire,
Without Narcissus' doom desire,
Serve without selfishness, and love
'Even as himself,' in sense above
Niggard 'as much,' yea, as she is
The only part of him that's his.

X
I do not say love's youth returns;
That joy which so divinely yearns!
But just esteem of present good
Shows all regret such gratitude
As if the sparrow in her nest,
Her woolly young beneath her breast,
Should these despise, and sorrow for
Her five blue eggs that are no more.
Nor say I the fruit has quite the scope
Of the flower's spiritual hope.
Love's best is service, and of this,
Howe'er devout, use dulls the bliss.
Though love is all of earth that's dear,
Its home, my Children, is not here:
The pathos of eternity
Does in its fullest pleasure sigh.

Be grateful and most glad thereof.
Parting, as 'tis, is pain enough.
If love, by joy, has learn'd to give
Praise with the nature sensitive,
At last, to God, we then possess
The end of mortal happiness,

And henceforth very well may wait
The unbarring of the golden gate,
Wherethrough, already, faith can see
That apter to each wish than we
Is God, and curious to bless
Better than we devise or guess;
Not without condescending craft
To disappoint with bliss, and waft
Our vessels frail, when worst He mocks
The heart with breakers and with rocks,
To happiest havens. You have heard
Your bond death-sentenced by His Word.
What, if, in heaven, the name be o'er,
Because the thing is so much more?
All are, 'tis writ, as angels there,
Nor male nor female. Each a stair
In the hierarchical ascent
Of active and recipient
Affections, what if all are both
By turn, as they themselves betroth
To adoring what is next above,
Or serving what's below their love?

Of this we are certified, that we
Are shaped here for eternity,
So that a careless word will make
Its dint upon the form we take
For ever. If, then, years have wrought
Two strangers to become, in thought,
Will, and affection, but one man
For likeness, as none others can,
Without like process, shall this tree
The king of all the forest, be,
Alas, the only one of all
That shall not lie where it doth fall?
Shall this unflagging flame, here nurs'd
By everything, yea, when reversed,
Blazing, in fury, brighter, wink,
Flicker, and into darkness shrink,
When all else glows, baleful or brave,
In the keen air beyond the grave?

Beware; for fiends in triumph laugh
O'er him who learns the truth by half!
Beware; for God will not endure
For men to make their hope more pure
Than His good promise, or require
Another than the five-string'd lyre
Which He has vow'd again to the hands
Devout of him who understands
To tune it justly here! Beware
The Powers of Darkness and the Air,

Which lure to empty heights man's hope,
Bepraising heaven's ethereal cope,
But covering with their cloudy cant
Its ground of solid adamant,
That strengthens ether for the flight
Of angels, makes and measures height,
And in materiality
Exceeds our Earth's in such degree
As all else Earth exceeds! Do I
Here utter aught too dark or high?
Have you not seen a bird's beak slay
Proud Psyche, on a summer's day?
Down fluttering drop the frail wings four,
Missing the weight which made them soar.
Spirit is heavy nature's wing,
And is not rightly anything
Without its burthen, whereas this,
Wingless, at least a maggot is,
And, wing'd, is honour and delight
Increasing endlessly with height.

XI

If unto any here that chance
Fell not, which makes a month's romance,
Remember, few wed whom they would.
And this, like all God's laws, is good;
For nought's so sad, the whole world o'er,
As much love which has once been more.
Glorious for light is the earliest love;
But worldly things, in the rays thereof,
Extend their shadows, every one
False as the image which the sun
At noon or eve dwarfs or protracts.
A perilous lamp to light men's acts!
By Heaven's kind, impartial plan,
Well-wived is he that's truly man
If but the woman's womanly,
As such a man's is sure to be.
Joy of all eyes and pride of life
Perhaps she is not; the likelier wife!
If it be thus; if you have known,
(As who has not?) some heavenly one,
Whom the dull background of despair
Help'd to show forth supremely fair;
If memory, still remorseful, shapes
Young Passion bringing Eshcol grapes
To travellers in the Wilderness,
This truth will make regret the less:
Mighty in love as graces are,
God's ordinance is mightier far;
And he who is but just and kind
And patient, shall for guerdon find,

Before long, that the body's bond
Is all else utterly beyond
In power of love to actualise
The soul's bond which it signifies,
And even to deck a wife with grace
External in the form and face.
A five years' wife, and not yet fair?
Blame let the man, not Nature, bear!
For, as the sun, warming a bank
Where last year's grass droops gray and dank,
Evokes the violet, bids disclose
In yellow crowds the fresh primrose,
And foxglove hang her flushing head,
So vernal love, where all seems dead,
Makes beauty abound.

Then was that nought,
That trance of joy beyond all thought,
The vision, in one, of womanhood?
Nay, for all women holding good,
Should marriage such a prologue want,
'Twere sordid and most ignorant
Profanity; but, having this,
'Tis honour now, and future bliss;
For where is he that, knowing the height
And depth of ascertain'd delight,
Inhumanly henceforward lies
Content with mediocrities!